HISTORY EDUCATION IN SCOTLAND

Into the New Millennium

Edited by Peter Hillis

JOHN DONALD PUBLISHERS LTD

EDINBURGH

ISBN 0 85976 515 6

British Library Cataloguing in Publication Data

A catalogue record for this book is available
from the British Library.

Typesetting and origination by Brinnoven, Livingston.
Printed and bound in Great Britain by J.W. Arrowsmith, Bristol.

Preface

I look back doun my centuries o life
To see the freindly grip
o Pict and Scot, when Kenneth and his wife
Plattit this kingrik up,
And whaur was desart, gart the gress grouw green.
And on Iona's isle
The white monks o Columcill I've seen,
And the santit bard himsel.

Hou sall aa the fowk I've been ere meet
And bide in yae wee house?
Knox wi Burns and Mary, Wishart and Beaton
Aa be snod and crouse?
Campbell and MacDonald be guid feirs,
The Bruis sup wi Comyn?
By God, I dout afore sic love appears,
Nae man sall kiss a woman!

Fergus, by Tom Scott

Tom Scott's poem, *Fergus*, illustrates Scotland's diverse and proud history. Scotland also has a long educational tradition, although at times this and its history have been uneasy bedfellows. In recent years History teachers have found themselves in the middle of controversies on a range of issues, notably the teaching of Scottish History and, more fundamentally, History's place in the Primary and Secondary curriculum. Nonetheless, many of today's History teachers have transformed the teaching of their subject. Gone is the old reliance on the standard textbook, lengthy teacher explanations and even lengthier dictated notes. In their place have come a wider variety of teaching methods and an emphasis on using primary and secondary sources. Commenting on one school, a report from Her Majesty's Inspector of Schools noted:

> Across the department there was a variety of methodology especially in Secondary
> 1 and Secondary 2. Video tapes, tape-slide presentations, debates, individual projects
> and maps were used along with effective class teaching to enliven pupils'

experience. A Secondary 2 class were achieving a high standard of discussion in deciding whether Mary, Queen of Scots was guilty of the murder of Lord Darnley. Individual projects from topics being studied involved pupils in conducting their own researches from an attractive range of books borrowed from the library and resource centre.[1]

If History teaches any lesson, it is that revolutions are circles, evidenced by recent educational debates focusing on 'knowledge deficits' and the merits of more traditional teacher-led methodologies. However, the report from Her Majesty's Inspector of Schools illustrates that good teaching uses a variety of approaches mixing the 'traditional' with the 'new'.

History teachers in Scotland have been in the vanguard of developments leading to changes in the ways in which pupils learn about the past. These changes now find parallels with current debates in both Europe and the United States of America. Scotland can contribute to and learn from these debates. This book, which draws on the experience of people working in Higher Education alongside Principal Teachers of History, aims to be part of this process. Moreover, the New Year is a time to reflect on the past and look forward to the future. This mixture of nostalgia and promise is more potent at the dawn of a new millennium providing an opportunity to chart the future progress for History Education.

Chapters 1–4 survey History's position in the curriculum and resultant pupil performance as demonstrated in external examinations. Chapters 5 and 6 offer comparative studies with analyses of developments in Europe and the United States of America. Chapters 7–12 concentrate on issues which will continue to inform debate about History Education, namely, meeting pupil needs, the principles underpinning syllabus design, the role of Information and Communication Technologies, teaching methodologies, using sources and arguments for and against the discrete teaching of History. One thing is certain, 'nae man sall kiss a woman' before historians stop debating their subject.

Notes

1. *Effective Learning and Teaching in Scottish Secondary Schools, History.* Scottish Office Education Department, 1992, p. 20.

Acknowledgements

The editor is indebted to Graham Holton for compiling the comprehensive index and to Elspeth Donaldson for typing the complete test.

The extract from Tom Scott's poem at the head of the Preface is reproduced by kind permission of his widow, and the cartoon on page 68 by permission of *Punch* library.

Notes on Contributors

Sandra Chalmers has been teaching since 1972. As Principal Teacher of History at Blantyre High School she became involved nationally in developing Standard Grade in the mid-1980s serving as Assistant Examiner 1992–99. She served on the National History Panel from 1987–92 and was a member of the working party for Revised Higher History. Sandra is joint author of the Standard Grade text *Scotland and Britain 1830–1980s*. She is now a joint setter for Intermediate 1 and 2. Sandra wants to make History exciting for young people.

David Duncan was educated at Stewart's Melville College, Aberdeen University and Queen's University in Canada, where he was a Commonwealth Scholar. He is a former Research Fellow at the University of the Witwatersrand, Johannesburg and is the author of two books on South African history. Besides working for the Scottish Consultative Council on the Curriculum as Director with responsibility for Corporate Affairs, he teaches an honours course in the Modern History Department at St Andrew's University.

Martin Feldman, a native New Yorker, began his professional career teaching Social Studies in secondary schools in New York City and then moved on to City University of New York. He took up a post at Jordanhill College of Education (now the Faculty of Education of the University of Strathclyde) in 1973. His major research interests are the social history of the USA, particularly Immigration, Education and Sport. Previous publications include *The Social Studies: Structure, Models, Strategies*, and various articles and book reviews in journals and newspapers on both sides of the Atlantic. He is currently a member of the History department at Strathclyde University.

Edmund J. Geraghty has been since 1974 Principal Teacher of History, John Ogilvie High School, Burnbank, South Lanark Education Authority. He is a former member of the Scottish Examination Board History Panel and a Setter for the Standard Grade Examination. He served on the Working Party which drew up the arrangements for Revised Higher History. At present he is a National Trainer in History for Higher Still.

Peter Hillis is Reader in History Education, Faculty of Education, University of Strathclyde. Before moving to Jordanhill he was Assistant Headteacher, Gleniffer High School, Paisley. He has served on the Scottish Qualifications Authority Subject Panel for History and is an Examiner for Intermediate 1 and 2 History within the Higher Still programme. Research interests include nineteenth- and twentieth-century Scottish religious History and the role of ICT in History Education.

Moira Laing taught History, Geography and Modern Studies at Dundee High School after graduating from St Andrew's and Glasgow Universities. After lecturing in Social

Studies at Hamilton College of Education she moved to Jordanhill where she is a Senior Lecturer in Primary Education and Programme Co-ordinator for Environment in the Faculty of Education. Her research and teaching interests include Environmental Education, Assessment in Environmental Studies 5–14 and Pre-Service Education (Primary).

Ian Matheson graduated from Glasgow University and the Australian National University. He taught at Cumbernauld High School before becoming Principal Teacher of History, first at Campbeltown Grammar School and then at Eastwood High School. He became Scottish Manager for Banking Information Service before moving to his present post as Chief Executive, Glasgow Colleges Group. Since 1991 he has been Principal Examiner for the Revised syllabus in Higher History. His publications include *People and Power: Germany 1918–1939* and *Passing Higher History: Skills for Success.*

James McGonigle has been Principal Teacher of History at Hermitage Academy, Helensburgh, since 1983. He is an honours graduate of the University of Glasgow having gained his degree in History and Economic History. He has a particular interest in the American Civil War and has researched the topic widely. He contributes regular book reviews to the *Times Educational Supplement Scotland* and is a member of various organisations, including the Scottish Association of Teachers of History and the Saltire Society.

Ian McKellar is Senior Lecturer in History in the Education Faculty of the University of Strathclyde and has considerable interests in History teaching and learning developments in a number of countries including the Netherlands, the Czech Republic, Estonia, Latvia, Georgia and Russia. He contributes also to the activities of EUROCLIO and the Council of Europe.

Bob Munro was formerly a Geography teacher and is now a Senior Lecturer in the Faculty of Education, University of Strathclyde. He has worked in the ICT field for over 15 years focusing on the integration of ICT into teaching/teacher education and the development of hypermedia resources. He has directed many national research initiatives and is currently involved in a Comenius Web project (with Iceland and Austria), an evaluation of ICT for the Scottish Council for Educational Technology and the delivery of an ICT training programme for Scottish teachers.

Duncan Toms is Principal Teacher of History, Bearsden Academy, East Dunbartonshire, having previously taught at Bellahouston Academy and St Gregory's Secondary, Glasgow. He is Convener of the Scottish Qualifications Authority History Panel, member of Higher Still History Specialist Group and writer of support materials for Higher and Intermediate levels on popular culture in Scotland 1880–1939. He is also a committee member of the Scottish Association of Teachers of History.

Sydney H. Wood was educated at Nelson Grammar School and Trinity College, Oxford. He was formerly Senior Lecturer in History at Northern College and currently holds a Teaching Fellowship at Dundee University. His particular interests include the relationship between school curricula and issues of national identity. He has been involved in all the national curricula initiatives affecting History in Scotland over the past 15 years. He is the author of numerous books and articles.

Contents

1

History in the Curriculum

Peter Hillis

The final four decades of the twentieth century have witnessed a growing debate over History's purpose and value in the school curriculum in contrast to the previous period when a general consensus existed over course content. John Slater characterised this content as:

> . . . largely British, or rather Southern English; Celts looked in to strave, emigrate or rebel; the North to invent looms or work in mills; abroad was of interest once it was part of the Empire; foreigners were either, sensibly, allies, or, rightly defeated. Skills – did we even use the word? – were mainly those of recalling accepted facts about famous dead Englishmen . . . It was an inherited consensus based largely on hidden assumptions, rarely identified let alone publicly debated.[1]

History syllabuses in Scotland could not escape criticisms of being excessively Anglocentric:

> . . . until the renaissance in Scottish historical studies of the past two to three decades, Scottish History was not widely taught in the Scottish universities or in schools.[2]

Beginning in the 1960s, a succession of authors challenged the traditional assumptions. In 1968 Mary Price's article 'History in Danger' argued that orthodox approaches to History education threatened its place in the curriculum.[3] Mary Price argued that History teachers had failed to justify their subject's place in the curriculum and, consequently, its aims were seen as increasingly irrelevant. Moreover, the over-concentration on British History and didactic teaching methods made History '. . . excruciatingly, dangerously dull, and, what is more, of little apparent relevance.'[4] Writing from a Scottish perspective John Fairley criticised the 'desperate race through the centuries to examine fleetingly the vicissitudes of fortune that befell an interminable procession of kings, barons, and archbishops (which) often provided the school learner with nothing beyond a set of imperfectly understood facts and ill digested notions . . .'.[5] Mary Price's article was followed by a series of publications which claimed that History's place in the curriculum remained under threat. Pamela Mays argued that History teaching was 'out of key with the age in which we live', while words, the medium of History, 'seem almost in disgrace' with '. . . people used to other easier and more superficially more attractive modes of communication.'[6] School History was attacked by some historians who believed that it was too difficult a subject to teach younger pupils since it required 'mature judgement, careful balancing of fact, meticulous attention to detail, abilities which children do not generally acquire until approaching adolescence.'[7] It was, therefore, hardly surprising some people advocated a course of Social Studies, or Civics, as being more relevant to the needs of pupils.

Many authors highlighted the dichotomy between the popularity of History as a leisure activity and its decline in schools. The adult audience has continued to expand evidenced by films, books, local enthusiasts and television. For example, *Time Team*, one of Channel 4's most popular programmes, is based on archaeology and History. Many adults who 'gladly escaped' from History at school 'return later to pursue her charms'.[8] For all her charms History could not protect against 'that great cultural shock of our age: rapid social change . . . which forces people into the future . . . about which History says little'.[9]

R.H.C. Davies warned of the dangers inherent in defending History education since the impression often conveyed was of an 'academic trade union . . . ensuring that the nation's education shall be so arranged that its members can go on teaching what they have always taught.'[10]. Moving History's image in more positive directions has been hindered by arguments over proposed solutions to reverse the downward trend and more fundamental disagreements over its aims in the school curriculum. Some of the proposed solutions failed to escape censure. John Chaffer and Lawrence Taylor criticised topics, projects and social studies as lacking the coherence which underpinned traditional courses resulting in a 'Steptoe and Son History, bright and attractive – but junk nonetheless.'[11]

Fundamental disagreements have focused on whether History has its own aims or aims subservient to the more general purposes of school education. John White claimed that History should further general educational objectives in promoting the well-being of students as 'autonomous i.e. self-determining members of a liberal democratic society.'[12] Autonomous people must have an understanding of the options from which choices are made, and the context within which these options exist. History illuminates these options and how aspects of present society have evolved. History can 'reveal to students strands in their own cultural background . . . that have helped to form their identity, to make them what they are'.[13] In the opposing corner Peter Lee expressed concerns that History may become distorted if used for specific political purposes. The justification for teaching History is not to change society but to change pupils, that is, to change their view of the world. School History should follow this aim rather than serving as a means to promote democratic citizenship, the danger being that it may cease to be History in becoming a form of indoctrination.[14] History should not serve as a method of social engineering; its role is to develop knowledge, understanding and skills.

Scotland pioneered many changes which radically altered History education. Mary Price's criticisms of History teaching were made in 1968, but Scotland had already begun to move in new directions. John Fairley led a series of changes which included activity methods, patch History and the use of museums and field studies. In his seminal work on activity methods, first published in 1967, John Fairley wrote:

> . . . the teacher will be prepared to introduce a fair method of flexibility into the work of the class. Oral lessons will have their place but much of their success will depend upon the extent to which they are followed up by the appropriate activity lessons. These can vary in form. Some children should be writing a simple story, whilst others compose a poem, a letter or a playlet . . . or there might be mixed-activity with some children making a model, some doing research from work cards, some preparing pictures for a frieze, and some experimenting.[15]

This quotation demonstrates the wider aspects of teaching and learning affected by changes to History education. The winds of change blew into many other areas including the demands of mixed-ability teaching, especially the needs of pupils requiring learning support,[16] and the use of primary historical sources. Traditional History syllabuses concentrated on increasing knowledge and understanding but in the 1960s greater attention was paid to the development of historical skills relating to investigating and evaluating, whereby pupils worked with primary historical sources. This development received official recognition in 1970 with the introduction of Alternative History Syllabuses for the middle and final stages of secondary schooling. In Alternative Ordinary Grade History 'each topic should be studied not only by the reading of textbooks but also by reference to source material and by encouraging acquaintance with literary and visual material related to that period'.[17] These developments laid the foundations for the present and foreseeable syllabuses discussed in this and other chapters.

Recent debates over History education in Scotland have concentrated on the position of national History rather than fundamental questions revolving around 'why teach History?' Scottish History has enjoyed a renaissance in recent years spurred on by a spectrum of developments ranging from films such as *Braveheart* to new and dynamic research in University History departments. Sydney Wood, a contributor to this volume, raised concerns over pupils' and student teachers' knowledge of Scottish History which sparked a national debate about its place in the overall History curriculum.[18] Implying that little or no Scottish History was taught, *The Sunday Times* claimed that 'Scottish History makes it back to the curriculum'.[19] By way of contrast, the *Times Educational Supplement* pronounced that '*Braveheart* fails to conquer curriculum'.[20] Pupils could have been forgiven for becoming concerned over the debate when other headlines stated, 'History pupils should do more homework'[21], and, 'Forsyth sets test on Scots History'.[22] History teachers remain divided over the 'Holywoodisation' of Scottish History with some arguing that it sparks pupil interest. 'I constantly have to convince pupils and their parents', declared Tom Monaghan, Principal Teacher of History at Stirling High School, 'that History is a useful and interesting subject. The Braveheart factor has undoubtedly helped'. Elizabeth Trueland, Principal Teacher of History at Mary Erskine School, took a more sceptical line in using 'the raised awareness of Scottish History that these films have brought to pupils to explore the issues of myths and reality; but you can be giving out confusing messages. They already come to class with quite strong preconceptions because of films'.[23] Responding to this debate the Scottish Consultative Council on the Curriculum commissioned a review group to report on Scottish History in the curriculum. In Chapter 8 of this book David Duncan analyses the debate and subsequent report which, reflecting the close inter-relationship between the rationale for History education and the choice of History topics, began by outlining the purposes of school History.[24]

Commenting on Scottish History in the curriculum Richard Finlay argued that it was 'about time . . . students (had) the opportunity to learn about Scottish History rather than a mainly anglicised British History.'[25] In a parallel twist to the debate Sylvia Collicott criticised a similar bias in the teaching of History in England. The predominantly anglo-centric approach should be replaced by child-centred methods requiring the teacher to recognise a 'diverse past and present and an ability to work outwards from these very differing perspectives.' Many teachers, claimed Sylvia Collicott, 'know that the content of the History curriculum is old-fashioned and out of touch with many of the interests of young people today. Particularly, teachers in inner city areas know that the History curriculum is culturally biased'.[26] In Chapters 5 and 6 Ian McKellar and Martin Feldman compare the debates and resulting curricula in Europe and North America to the Scottish situation.

For the harassed History teacher debates over purpose, aims and content can appear esoteric, since they often appear to neglect the realities in schools, with the subject receiving a shrinking share of the timetable, and an audience of whom some remain stubbornly unmoved by History's charms. This chapter sets History education in the context of the overall Scottish curriculum and suggests a rationale to carry the subject forward into the new millennium.

Curriculum Context

In Scotland most pupils begin formal schooling at the age of 5 years with entry in Primary 1. Primary schooling continues until Primary 7, pupil age

11 years, after which pupils move into the first year of Secondary School. Secondary Schools have six stages although some students opt to leave school when reaching 16 years of age, the statutory leaving age. However, an increasing number of students stay on at school beyond the statutory leaving age partly due to high levels of youth unemployment but also resulting from increased expectations by society for formal educational qualifications. The introduction of Higher Still courses is likely to increase staying on rates into the early 2000s as schools provide a wider range of courses at different levels.

Number of Primary Schools	Number of Primary 7 Pupils	Number of Secondary Schools	Numbers of Pupils By Stages in Secondary Schools					
			S1	S2	S3	S4	S5	S6
2,386	64,108	463	62,958	62,481	62,937	64,842	51,851	28,864

Table 1.1: Numbers of Primary 7 Pupils and Numbers of Pupils in Secondary Schools by Stages, 1996.[27]

In 1994, 24,345 teachers were employed in Secondary Schools and of this total, 1,379 taught History. This total compared to 1,176 Geography and 791 Modern Studies teachers. Teachers of History, and all other subjects in both Primary and Secondary Schools, operate within general curriculum guidelines laid down by the Scottish Consultative Council on the Curriculum. The guidelines, which are being revised, will take schools into the millennium. The draft guidelines divide the curriculum into between 5 and 8 modes, one of which, Social and Environmental Studies, includes History from Secondary 3 to Secondary 6.[28] However, in Secondary 1 and Secondary 2 one mode encompasses Science, Technology and Society, an unnatural alliance of subjects which threatens History's position in the early years of Secondary school. A discrete mode for Social and Environmental Studies should also feature in Secondary 1 and 2.

Unlike the National Curriculum in England, History syllabuses in Scotland retain a degree of flexibility and teacher choice regarding course content. The national programme for Primary 1 to Secondary 2, pupil ages 5–14 years, contains History within Environmental Studies and lays down general guidelines for courses. Table 1.2 compares Scottish and English syllabuses for the age range 5–14 years.

The Scottish guidelines cover similar historical eras to the National Curriculum but do not specify topics within the stipulated time periods. Within the Ancient World schools opt for a range of studies, including Skara Brae and/or Ancient Egypt, but in the National Curriculum Ancient Greece must be taught. As Moira Laing and Duncan Toms argue in Chapters 2 and 3 this flexibility has an advantage in retaining an element of teacher choice but

PROGRAMME OF STUDY – SCOTLAND	PROGRAMME OF STUDY – KEY STAGE 2 ENGLAND
A. Studies selected from each era: The Ancient World; Renaissance, Reformation and the Age of Discovery; The Middle Ages; The Age of Revolution; The Twentieth Century.	Romans, Anglo-Saxons and Vikings in Britain Life in Tudor Times Victorian Britain Britain since 1930 Ancient Greece Local History A Past Non-European Society
B Some studies which trace developments across time.	PROGRAMME OF STUDY - KEY STAGE 3
C Within A and B, Scottish contexts, one British, one European and one non-European context.	Britain 1066–1500 The Making of the United Kingdom: Crowns, Parliaments and Peoples 1800–1750 Britain 1750–circa 1900
ATTAINMENT TARGETS	The Twentieth-Century World An Era or Turning Points in European
Knowledge and Understanding Planning Collecting Evidence Recording and Presenting Interpreting and Evaluating Developing Informed Attitudes	History Before 1914 A Past Non-European Society. KEY ELEMENTS Chronology Range and Depth of Historical Understanding Interpretations of History Historical Enquiry Organisation and Communication

Table 1.2: History Syllabuses in Scotland Primary 1 to Secondary 2, and England Year Groups 3 to 9.[29]

the disadvantage of making it more difficult to target resources. Standard Grade History, the national History course in Secondary 3 and 4 (pupil ages 14–15 years), retains this flexible approach in providing a choice of contexts within three compulsory units. For example, Unit 1, Changing Life in Scotland and Britain, contains three contexts, one of which must be studied: 1750s–1850s or 1830s–1930s or 1880s to Present Day.[30] In Secondary 5 and 6 the History syllabuses within the Higher Still programme provide a wide choice of time periods and studies therein. In Higher History, one of the four levels of Higher Still courses, departments choose one from Medieval, Early Modern and Later Modern options, within which a further range of choices is provided. In the Later Modern option one topic must be selected from:

Patterns of Migration: Scotland 1830s–1930s;
Appeasement and the Road to War to 1939;
The Origins and Development of the Cold War 1945–1985;
Ireland 1900–1985: A Divided Identity.[31]

6

The attainment targets noted in Table 2 highlight the trend towards investigative approaches in teaching and learning History. Within the target, Planning, pupils choose an issue to investigate leading into the attainment targets of collecting evidence and recording/presenting. This approach necessitates using a range of primary and secondary sources which must also be evaluated against such criteria as authorship, bias and expressed points of view. The skill of evaluating features in every national History course, for example, at Standard Grade pupils must evaluate sources 'with reference to their historical significance, the points of view conveyed in them and to the relevant historical context'.[32] As Eddie Geraghty discusses in Chapter 11, the use of sources requires careful planning but can play an important role in developing pupils' literary skills. While evaluating features as a consistent element within History courses at every level the approach to investigating is more fragmented. The attainment targets within Environmental Studies 5–14, the Extended Essay/Response At Higher and Intermediate 2, and the Dissertation in Advanced Higher all involve an investigative methodology. However, from 1999 the dropping of the Standard Grade Historical Investigation in Secondary 3 and 4 removed an important bridge between investigative skills in Upper Primary, Secondary 1 and 2 and Secondary 5 and 6. As Duncan Toms speculates in Chapter 3 this may lead to a realignment of History courses early in the new millennium.

Debates over course content cannot ignore the reality of History being only one of several subjects within the Social and Environmental Studies mode which includes Geography, Modern Studies and Classical Studies. The Scottish Consultative Council on the Curriculum recommends that the Environmental Studies mode receives a minimum 10 per cent of time available in S1 and S2. This translates into a normal allocation of one period, 55 minutes, per week during S1 and S2 and, as discussed by Duncan Toms in Chapter 3, this time allowance restricts the aims of History education. In Chapter 2 Moira Laing notes similar time constraints in the Primary Curriculum. The aims and rationale for History education must take cognisance of the very limited amount of time which History receives in the curriculum. Nonetheless, this book argues that History's rationale and ability to contribute towards active citizenship present a powerful case for increased time in both the Primary and Secondary curriculum.

From Secondary 3 (pupil age 14) History becomes an optional subject, set against the other social subjects as illustrated by the typical range of subject choices shown in Table 1.3.

Table 1.4 shows the number of pupils presented for Standard Grade History, Higher History and the Certificate of Sixth Year Studies, the national courses in Secondary 5 and Secondary 6 (pupil ages 16–17 years). Presentations for English provide a basis for year group comparison with figures for Geography

7

Column A	Column B	Column C	Column D	Column E	Column F	Column G	Column H	Column I
English	Mathematics	French German	Geography History Modern Studies	Biology Chemistry Physics Standard- Science	Art Biology Computing Craft & Design Geography Home-Economics Office and Information Studies Physics Technical Studies	Accounting & Finance Art Chemistry Computing Craft & Design Graphic - Communication Home Economics Music Physical Education	Art Computing German Home-economics Keyboard Skills Musical - Keyboard P.E. - (Gymnastics) Technical	Art Computing European-Studies Finance Record- Keeping French Home-Economics Music Technical

Table 1.3: Subject Choice Secondary 2 into Secondary 3.

and Modern Studies demonstrating the relative popularity of History as a social subject.

Subject	Standard Grade	Higher	Certificate of Sixth Year Studies
English	62,604	32,057	15,28
History	21,99	6,840	574
Geography	25,102	9,068	355
Modern Studies	14,447	7,154	339

Table 1.4: Number of Pupils Presented for Standard Grade, Higher and Certificate of Sixth-Year Studies History, Geography, Modern Studies and English. 1996[33]

In Chapter 4 Ian Matheson analyses pupil performance in these examinations but these statistics, which remained relatively constant throughout the 1990s, show that approximately 66 per cent of pupils stop studying History at the end of Secondary 2 with a further declining percentage at the transition from Standard Grade into Higher. Moreover, within the social subjects History is not the most popular option at Standard Grade and Higher for reasons which, as Sydney Wood argues in Chapter 7, partly relate to pupil perceptions of the subject. Consequently, the aims and rationale of History education operate in the context of a subject which most pupils no longer study beyond 14 years of age.

A Rationale for History Education

The heading for this section states 'a' rationale rather than 'the' rationale since there is no simple or single rationale for History education. The old cliché of two historians but three opinions is both a strength and a weakness in promoting the subject. The cliché highlights the difficulty in reaching a consensus over aims and rationale which range from Marxist economic determinism to Collingwood's 'attempt to get inside the mind of the individual.'[34] As noted below, the historian's ability to reach conclusions from a range of evidence is a valuable skill, but an excess of what can appear as an introverted debate over its purpose may leave History sidelined by other subjects in the curriculum. History requires a clearer rationale as the new millennium approaches if it is successfully to market its worth.

The relatively small proportion of pupils opting to study History beyond Secondary 2 contrasts with its popularity as a leisure activity. As Sydney Wood demonstrates, many pupils regard History as a relatively difficult subject. The common reply to hearing that someone is a History teacher: 'Oh, I hated it at school – all dates and battles.'[35] Pupil choice is partly influenced by the small number of direct employment opportunities leading from History qualifications, but a prerequisite for any History course in schools is that it should be an enjoyable and interesting experience. This is particularly important for those pupils who cease studying History in Secondary 2 since they will retain a general impression of the subject rather than detailed knowledge. Many pupils have a pragmatic approach to schooling and 'a degree of resistance or indifference to some of the more arcane aspects of History . . . interest, relevance and accessibility are the sine qua non of teaching History in ordinary schools.'[36] In her justification for teaching History Marjorie Reeves concluded:

> Yet the last word here must be enjoyment. Even the tragedy of History is to be enjoyed . . .'[37]

'The correct sentiment, but the wrong order of priority' could be a teacher's comment on this statement since enjoyment and interest deserve a higher rating. The report into Scottish History in the curriculum outlined the general characteristics of successful History education which 'to be truly effective must capture young people's imagination and stimulate their interest. This is the first and arguably the most important characteristic of effective History education in schools.'[38] The challenge for schools is to capitalise on History's popularity in higher education and as a leisure activity. This will necessitate a move away from the current over-emphasis on assessment to allow a far greater concentration on developing innovative teaching materials and methods such as those described by Sandra Chalmers in Chapter 10. These make learning enjoyable and relevant and help increase pupil numbers beyond Secondary 2. The aim should be to help pupils 'acquire an interest in the past [which] is itself a cultural acquisition which can enrich the whole of one's adult life. It can become an abiding pleasure and a source of intellectual satisfaction.'[39]

A rationale which emphasises enjoyment and interest may be regarded as a justification for 'edutainment'. History courses need not apologise for entertaining pupils, if this equates with enjoyment, but the 'edu' element of 'edutainment' encompasses the development of knowledge and understanding alongside historical skills, many of which transfer to other subjects and careers. According to Hegel, History teaches us that peoples and governments never learned anything from History, or acted on principles deduced from it. Nonetheless, helping people understand the present through studying the past remains central to the rationale for History education. Many post Second World War crises have been influenced by the perception of events in the 1930s. In a broadcast to the American people during the Cuban missile crisis, President John F. Kennedy claimed that:

The 1930s taught us a clear lesson. Aggressive conduct, if allowed to go unchecked and unchallenged ultimately leads to war.[49]

In August 1990, six days after the Iraqi invasion of Kuwait, President George Bush echoed President Kennedy's assertion:

If History teaches us anything it is that we must resist aggression or it will destroy our freedoms. Appeasement does not work.[41]

During the 1990s demands have increased for the restitution of mistakes in the past with many associated symbols and people under attack. For example, leaders of the black community in Bristol demanded the removal of Edward Colson's statue since he had made his fortune from the triangular trade.[42] With a commanding view over Sutherland's east coast, the statue of the Duke of Sutherland symbolises, for many people, the injustices of the Highland Clearances.[43] History's role in illuminating the past and the present comes in several parts. Through explaining causes and effects of changes in the past it contributes to a sense of perspective essential to an understanding of the present day. It helps to create an individual's self belief and sense of belonging to a society with a past constantly changing over time. Part of this sense of belonging involves an understanding of societies' values but this does not assume that there are shared values or that values have been and/or are valuable. History does not seek to impose a value system on pupils but it allows pupils to examine how past values influenced people's actions and the ways which many of these values continue to influence the present. However, it sets in context present debates over social justice and aims to promote confidence in active citizenship through an appreciation that many of the ideas, values and institutions which are sometimes taken for granted were often created by the sacrifices of individuals, groups and peoples. Similar sacrifices may be necessary in the future.

Acquiring historical knowledge remains a prerequisite for developing historical skills and an understanding of key concepts such as cause and effect. The selection of course content is, therefore, central to planning but choice must be based upon transparent principles. Moreover, pupils and parents should be informed as to the topics being taught and the justification for this selection. Scottish syllabuses have been criticised for an over concentration on German History between the World Wars but this topic shows how a democracy can be destroyed under certain circumstances with results far beyond the immediate situation. A successful future for History education partly depends on this, and other justifications, being clearly explained to pupils and parents.

History syllabuses should allow for the progressive development of knowledge and understanding across a wide range of time from early History to the twentieth century. Topics should encompass Scottish, British, European and World History covering political, social, economic and cultural themes. A balanced and flexible approach should continue allowing teachers to select within general parameters topics which interest both themselves and pupils. The teacher's knowledge and enthusiasm for a topic remains the strongest selling point for History. Consequently, a national History curriculum in Scotland would be a backward step and a growing cause for concern is uniform courses brought on by the requirement of the 5–14 programme. Faced with multiplying demands for planning, assessment, recording and reporting teachers increasingly look to pre-prepared, often commercially produced, units. The six strands for the social subjects within Environmental Studies 5–14, knowledge and understanding, planning, collecting evidence, recording and presenting, interpreting and evaluating and developing informed attitudes, contain over 140 attainment targets to be assessed between Primary 1 and Secondary 2.[44] One challenge for the millennium is to topple assessment from its pre-eminent position, replacing it with a concentration on the quality of teaching, learning and resources.

John Slater observed that 'History pupils who appear to know little do not make a good case for its teaching.'[45] Support for this observation came in the negative publicity following a survey which revealed a 'knowledge deficit' in pupils' understanding of Scottish History.[46] An appreciation of History begins with secure knowledge but a rationale extends into developing skills, some unique to History, but others which transfer into wider applications. Higher Still courses must include the core skills of:

PERSONAL EFFECTIVENESS AND PROBLEM-SOLVING SKILLS

Critical thinking
Planning and organising
Reviewing and evaluating
Working in teams

COMMUNICATION

Oral communication (including use of images)
Written communication (including use of images)

NUMERACY

Using graphical information
Using number

INFORMATION TECHNOLOGY

Using information technology[47]

Historians can relate most of these core skills with historical skills but they must convince school managers, employers, students and parents that, for example, critical thinking and written communication are developed by studying History. In Chapter 9, Bob Munro demonstrates how History can make a significant contribution towards delivering information technology across the curriculum. History enhances the 'use of language, numeracy, observation and communication.'[48] This raises fundamental questions when it is advocated that the time given to History, especially in Primary Schools, should be reduced and re-allocated to English and Mathematics in the drive to increase language and numeracy standards. The need for this re-allocation raises issues relevant to the teaching of English and Mathematics rather than the time given to History.

Debates surrounding the use in History education of films such as *Braveheart* raise fundamental issues relating to aims and rationale. Pupils may question the relevance of a History course which ignores the genre of film. To be fully effective History teaching must develop skills in analysing and evaluating information by detecting inaccuracies, bias and propaganda. The English army's tactics at the Battle of Stirling Bridge in crossing the River Forth at one place, Stirling Bridge, played a crucial role in Wallace's victory. History and Hollywood have always been awkward partners as evidenced by the depiction of the Battle of Stirling Bridge in *Braveheart* where the Bridge did not exist. History aims to develop a healthy scepticism in an age increasingly dominated by the media and spin doctors. As the new millennium approaches, people are confronted with an increasing volume of information and it is the role of the History teacher to educate young people 'to sort out the differences between essential and non-essential information, raw fact, prejudice, lay-truth and untruth, so that they know when they are being manipulated, by whom, and for what purpose.'[49]

Other subjects could claim a similar rationale but History claims a singular contribution to learning since it helps pupils understand the past and present in unique ways and contexts. Historical truth finds its roots in evidence while accepting the validity of alternative points of view. A teaching style which accepts these differing opinions provides a model for pupils to follow. Nonetheless, as John Slater emphasises, expectations must be realistic given the age of pupils and time available in the curriculum.

> [History] cannot guarantee tolerance, though it can give it some intellectual weapons. It cannot keep open closed minds, although, it may, sometimes, leave a nagging grain of doubt in them. Historical thinking is primarily mind-opening, not socialising . . . thinking historically is a strand in the fabric of national thought which must be jealously and urgently defended.[50]

Developing these attitudes within a knowledge of the past provides a persuasive justification for History education and cautions against integrated social subjects. Jim McGonigle expands on this theme in Chapter 12.

However valid the above rationale, many parents and pupils look towards future careers when choosing subjects. *Why Study History? History and Choosing Your Career*, published by the Historical Association, lists 87 careers where History is either demanded, actively sought or a useful enhancement.[51] These careers range from archaeology and architecture to retail distribution and town planning. Many History graduates succeed in other careers and acknowledge the value of historical skills. The variety of skills and knowledge imparted through the study of History will become increasingly important in changing career structures and government encouragement to lifelong learning. An appreciation of technological change in the past sets in context the impact of present and future technologies.

Conclusion

Individuals, societies and nations cannot escape their past. Scotland's psyche is embedded in its History. The Wars of Independence, Mary Queen of Scots, the Highland Clearances, the Scottish Enlightenment, Industrialisation and the economic blizzards of the 1980s stretch out to influence present attitudes and values. History is presented with a golden opportunity to enhance its place in the Primary and Secondary curriculum as Scotland prepares for the most important constitutional change since the Act of Union. However, for evangelisation to succeed History education requires a clear vision as to what it expects to achieve, and how to achieve it. The knowledge and skills developed through historical study assume greater importance in a society undergoing rapid social, economic and political change, but it will require vigorous promotion to ensure that History education remains of fundamental importance in the curriculum and is seen by society in general to justify this position. Comparing the position of Latin and Greek in the school curriculum between 1970 and 2000 warns against any complacency regarding the future well-being of History education.

Notes

1. John Slater, *The Politics of History Teaching, A Humanity, Dehumanized?*. (London, 1988), p.1.
2. Scottish History in the Curriculum. A Statement of Position from Scottish CCC. Scottish Consultative Council on the Curriculum, 1998, p.12.
3. Mary Price, 'History in Danger', *Teaching History*, No. 179, November, 1968.
4. Ibid.
5. John Fairley, *Patch History and Creativity*, (Longman, 1970), p.7
6. Pamela Mays, *Why Teach History?* (London, 1974), p.1.

7. Ibid.

8. Marjorie Reeves, *Why History?* (Longman, 1980), p.2.

9. Ibid.

10. R.H.C. Davis, 'Why Have an Historical Association?', *History*, Vol. 58, No. 193, 1973.

11. John Chaffer and Lawrence Taylor, *History and the History Teacher*, (London, 1975), p.15.

12. John White, 'The Aims of School History', *Teaching History*, Vol. 74, January 1994.

13. Ibid.

14. See, for example, Peter Lee 'Historical Knowledge and the National Curriculum' in H. Bourdillon (ed) *Teaching History*, (London, 1994).

15. John Fairley, *Activity Methods in History*, (Nelson, 1967), p.5. See also by the same author *Patch History and Creativity*, (Longman, 1970) and *History Teaching Through Museums*, (Longman, 1977).

16. See for example G.F. Gold, *Pupils with Learning Difficulties in History*, Jordanhill College of Education, 1982.

17. Alternative Ordinary Grade History, Scottish Examination Board, Examination Arrangements, 1970, p.153.

18. Sydney Wood, 'Trapped in the Dark Ages', *Times Educational Supplement*, 31/5/1996.

19. *The Sunday Times*, 13/10/1996.

20. *Times Educational Supplement*, 18/10/1996.

21. *The List*, No. 292, 1996.

22. *The Sunday Times*, 26/1/1997.

23. Fiona MacLeod, 'History According to Holyrood or Hollywood', *Times Educational Supplement*, 13/2/1998.

24. Scottish History In the Curriculum, A Paper for Discussion and Consultation, Scottish Consultative Council on the Curriculum, 1997, p.3–4.

25. *The Sunday Times*, 26/1/1997.

26. Sylvia Collicott, 'Who Is the National Curriculum For?' *Teaching History*, No. 61, October, 1990.

27. Statistics quoted in this chapter were provided by the Scottish Office Education and Industry Department.

28. Curriculum Design for the Secondary Stages, Guidelines for Schools. Consultative Draft, Scottish Consultative Council on the Curriculum, 1998, p. 59–61.

29. For Scotland see Curriculum Assessment in Scotland National Guidelines Environmental Studies 5–14, Scottish Office Education Department, 1993, p.34–35 and 38–45. Table 2 refers to Key Stages 2 and 3, pupil ages 7–14 years,

of History in the National Curriculum, Department for Education, 1995, p.4–17.

30. Scottish Certificate of Education, Standard Grade Arrangements in History, Scottish Qualifications Authority, 1997, p.10.

31. Higher Still Arrangements for History, Higher Still Development Unit, 1997, p.5.

32. Standard Grade Arrangements for History, p.9.

33. Examination Statistics, 1996, Scottish Examination Board, (Edinburgh, 1997).

34. John Chaffer and Lawrence Taylor, *History and the History Teacher*, (London, 1975), p.24.

35. Marjorie Reeves, *Why History?* p.1.

36. Terry Haydn, James Arthur and Martin Hunt, *Learning to Teach History in the Secondary School*, p.14.

37. Marjorie Reeves, *Why History?* p.47.

38. Scottish History in the Curriculum, p.4.

39. Keith Joseph, Why Teach History in School? *The Historian*, Vol. 2, 1989.

40. Quoted in Alex Danchev 'Cold War Crisis in Camelot', *Times Higher Education Supplement*, 16/1/1988.

41. Ibid.

42. *The Times*, 29/1/1998.

43. *The Herald*, 6/4/1998.

44. Environmental Studies 5–14, p.38–45 and National Guidelines 5–14 Level F, Consultation Document, 1997, p.1–5.

45. John Slater, 'The Case for History in Schools', *The Historian*, No. 2, 1984.

46. See, for example, Tom Devine, 'History Knowledge is Behind the Times', *Scotsman*, 25/2/1998.

47. Higher Still: Core Skills: Further Consultation Document. Higher Still Development Unit, 1996, p.9

48. Keith Joseph, 'Why Teach History?'

49. N. Longworth, 'We're Moving Into the Information Society – What Shall We Tell the Children?' *Computer Education*, June, 1981.

50. John Slater, 'The Politics of History Teaching, A Humanity Dehumanized?'

51. *Why Study History?* is available from the Historical Association, 590 Kenington Park Road, London SE11 4JH.

2

History Education in Primary Schools

Moira Laing

The 'Past' Dimension in Environmental Studies 5–14

Primary teachers are concerned, not just with History education, but with the delivery of an effective Environmental Studies curriculum of which History is an integral part. Although the 5–14 guidelines shy away from referring directly to History, the subject is undeniably there as Understanding People in the Past making a distinctive contribution to this complex and wide-ranging curriculum area. Together with People and Place and People in Society, this outcome provides a framework in which to debate, select and devise people-focused studies, long cherished as classroom favourites by primary pupils and teachers alike.

This past dimension is clearly a prerequisite for extending the scope of Environmental Studies featuring prominently in the initial definition of what environment means in the 5–14 curriculum:

> The environment . . . encompasses all the social, physical and cultural conditions which influence, or have influenced, the lives of the individual and community and which shape, or have been shaped by, the actions, artefacts and institutions of successive generations.[1]

Consequently, the past dimension clearly contributes to fulfilling the three fundamental aims expressed in the rationale for Environmental Studies, namely that:

(a) the environment should provide a context for learning
(b) pupils should understand their environment
(c) the environment is important.

With its focus upon studies of People, Events and Societies of Significance in the Past, this outcome can provide a range of rich contexts for learning by developing young people's awareness and understanding of their own communities, helping them to interpret and make sense of others distant in place and time, extending and deepening their experiences and insights into other people's values, actions and ways of life. For many years studies of the past in Primary Schools were perceived as particularly rich contexts for learning but rather too often for enhancing skills in Language and Expressive

Arts than for developing an understanding of people, events and societies. Now that the 5–14 guidelines have swept that traditional practice aside, legitimate past studies have excellent potential for illuminating pupils' learning concerned as they are with investigating every aspect of any society – its art, stories, music, technology, science, religious beliefs and practices.

Approaches to studying the past which stimulate the imagination and actively involve pupils as investigators, as well as a judicious selection of contexts, go a long way towards enabling young people to understand their environment. If the school follows the 5–14 guidelines as a structure for learning, 'pupils will . . . be helped to understand the social, economic, cultural, physical and technological factors operating on their environment and the relationships among these factors'. Such understanding will 'grow to encompass other places and times . . . pointing pupils to Scottish, British, European and global dimensions'.[2] Recurring comparisons between our past and present society are both relevant and revealing to young pupils. The major issue for every Scottish school is to determine what constitutes the best selection of past studies 'to provide young people with a map of the past which will help them to understand the inheritance and identity of their own society and that of other societies'.[3] Throughout the 1990s, a strong lobby of professional and public opinion has steadily grown giving voice to the argument that a Scottish narrative should be central to any programme of studies of the past. Pupils then will understand how their nation evolved and what Scots contributed to human endeavour and achievements in British and in wider world cultures, giving them as inheritors a sense of national identity and self-worth.

A school's programme in Environmental Studies should lead pupils to recognise that the environment is crucially important for many reasons – survival, quality of lifestyle, benefits of interdependence, the wisdom deriving from its inheritance – and society must take active responsibility for its care and conservation. Pupils should be able to interpret how 'events, decisions and changes made in the past have shaped the existing environment' and recognise that, as 'today's children [they] will contribute to the shaping of the environment of the future'.[4] Studies of the past are obviously perceived to make a very particular and direct contribution to fostering informed, responsible and active citizenship. In the process of investigating past societies, pupils will touch upon many social and cultural issues still pertinent today, have opportunities to empathise with others and learn how, and why, people's values, attitudes and viewpoints then may differ from their own today. A well structured programme of Scottish contexts in particular should 'contribute to the sense of belonging, a respect and care for others and a sense of social responsibility which Scottish Schools are now actively seeking to promote at a multiplicity of levels'.[5]

In the overall 5–14 curriculum context the personal and social development of each individual is a strong permeating element which is becoming increasingly explicit in classroom practice. In *History in the Early Years*, Hilary Cooper asserts that, even for very young children, History is an 'essential' focus for holistic development.[6] Studying people in the past and making comparisons with an increasingly familiar present lead young people to make links between themselves and others, between school and community, between past, present and future, between change and continuity. It links imagination with deductive reasoning and, in so doing, develops initiative, independent and critical thinking and a growing sense of moral awareness. To think historically, involving as it does both asking and responding to such questions as, 'What would it be like to live like that? Why did people do/think that? How do I know that this is what happened?', contributes very substantially not only to the cognitive development of young pupils but to their social and emotional maturity as well.

'Understanding People in the Past' as History

The Key Features of People in the Past have at times aroused stronger feelings among the teaching profession, and the public, than any other element in the 5–14 curriculum. This guideline for History education endorses that knowledge, skills and attitudes all matter and sets out a general framework for progressive programmes of study at each of the stages, Primary 1 to Primary 3, Primary 4 to Primary 6, Primary 7 to Secondary 2. Peter Hillis, in Chapter 1, summarises the broad range of historical study from 5 to 14 which sets the parameters for such programmes in Scottish schools, contrasting the guideline framework with the prescribed content base of History in the National Curriculum.

While the 5–14 guidelines present a more comprehensive idea than most previous documentation of what studies of the past should be targeting in primary classrooms with a welcome emphasis on contexts and content for developing understanding, they do not specify, or even hint at, any core of studies which could best promote learning across the five stipulated eras. There is no real debate within the guidelines as to what knowledge should be taught and a restricted view of the attitudes which could be informed and developed through investigating past societies. Consequently, pupils across Scotland study a range of discrete topics or units in more, or less, depth which, because of a very tight timescale, must inevitably contain gaps, significant to many, resulting in a patchy knowledge base which may fall short of providing a real sense of the long time line of the Scottish or British story. These and other concerns have led to the current review of Environmental Studies 5–14.

The justification for such flexibility of choice would argue that schools should take their own decisions about the selection of studies based on their particular appropriateness to the local community, to the use of adjacent historical sites and human sources, and to teachers' preferences reflecting personal interest, academic background, professional experiences and/or familiarity with a potentially fruitful resource-base. In tune with this reasoning, pupils should perceive studies of the past as dynamic and relevant in that they illuminate changes and effects in their own community or country and are delivered in meaningful and exciting ways by enthusiastic teachers. While this can certainly be the case, the fact that no core of studies, Scottish-based or otherwise, exists across the country presents a significant resource problem for schools. It also proliferates the tension of Primary 7 to Secondary 1 liaison and causes anxiety amongst teachers as to what studies are 'best' to teach and how to deal with the inevitable 'gaps'. All of these problems are particularly acute when planning and implementation time for studies of the past is at a premium.

The public, too, have shown strength of feeling about the lack of direction as to what should be studied in People in the Past. Some claim that pupils are taught how to be historians but know less and less about what actually happened and certainly not why.[7] The fact that there is no real debate to assist the selection of a Scottish core of studies is out of step both with other nations who have distinct national stories built into their curricula and with the vigorous academic interest in Scottish History in the 1990s.[8] The Scottish History Review Group see the pupils' essential 'map of the past' as something which 'has to be built up over time, as young people develop the maturity to deal with more sophisticated concepts and interpretations of historical events and processes.'[9] Yet it is claimed that the young people emerging from our schools today run the risk of having a disjointed sense of History with no firm base of understanding on which to anchor new experiences and address the future.

One 'baffled' correspondent speaks for parental concerns on this matter particularly cogently. Because, in their experience, some children through Primary into Secondary 'dipped' in and out of a plethora of studies, they had in the end 'no sense of international cause and effect – nor an awareness of progression of any kind'. They could recall few dates from Scottish History and had no clue about how their inheritance 'had moved on from earth mounds to cathedrals to telecottages. They had no sense of the passage of time, no sense of their own place in History'.[10] Sufficient concern is expressed both within the profession and the general public to render this a very serious situation indeed, particularly when, for the majority of pupils, an interpretation of 'People in the Past' is the only History they may ever experience in their formal education.

Guidelines by their very nature require interpretation by the user with subsequent translation into practical contexts for learning. Selecting studies and justifying a coherent and progressive programme from Primary 1 to Secondary 2 is a challenge for anyone, including the specialist historian. Primary teachers are not usually historians and their specialism is their generalist function of effective delivery of the total 5–14 curriculum to a specific primary class. Consequently, while it can be argued that this is a healthy professional situation to find themselves in, primary teachers have much to think about as they take such fundamental decisions about this one element in a curriculum which increasingly bristles with priorities. Drawing upon their own and their colleagues' subject and pedagogical knowledge, as a staff they require to find answers to some very important questions:

(a) What studies are most 'significant' for our pupils – and why?
(b) What should primary children be learning about the past – and why?
(c) To what extent are we teaching knowledge of the past and/or the historian's perspective and way of working?
(d) How can younger pupils learn about the past? What kinds of activities can we develop to promote this learning?

Presumably, in recognition of some of the shortcomings of the guidelines and the need to provide clearer direction on some of the issues contained in these questions, the Scottish Consultative Council on the Curriculum published exemplification of all outcomes in Environmental Studies 5–14, of which Understanding People in the Past is one of the most substantially detailed.[11] While it goes little further in prescribing what should be studied – indeed, it stresses that the examples it illustrates 'should not be regarded as in any sense offering prescriptive models of good practice', nor do they 'prescribe particular teaching approaches' – it does provide clarification on how to interpret and use the key features and audit programmes of past studies.[12] In its practical analysis of each key feature it emphasises a variety of ways in which effective learning about the past can be planned for and provides some criteria, at least, upon which progression can be tracked and developed.

This exemplification document identifies the two key features, 'studying people, events and societies of significance in the past' and 'considering the meaning of heritage', as the features 'which condition the choice of relevant topics to be undertaken and which ensure breadth and balance of coverage across study programmes'.

Other than a few exemplars of topics which illustrate planning processes, there is no further debate on what could constitute essential or desirable core studies, although the rationale for choice is clearly confirmed.

As an audit mechanism, however, this publication does open up a helpful dialogue with schools, providing through its questions a checklist whereby they can evaluate, then confirm or adjust what they currently do or intend to

Broad Stage Primary 1 to Primary 3	
CONTEXT OF STUDY Emphasising: • pupils' own experience and own past. • immediate environment and its past. • stories about the past.	CONTENT OF STUDIES To include: • pupils' own past and past of their families and communities. • memories • significant events • stories developing awareness of the past.
Broad Stages Primary 4 to Primary 6 and Primary 7 to Secondary 2	
CONTEXT OF STUDY Pupils' own experience is still important, but there should be gradual extension of study to encompass studies of: • five specified periods (see page 34 of the Guidelines) • Scottish, British, European, non-European contexts • long-term developments in e.g. farming, housing. • important events and contributions of individual people • how past events have significant effects on present societies • political, economic, social, cultural aspects of History.	CONTENT OF STUDIES • distinctive historical features of periods or topics in studies of the past • diversity of lifestyles and experiences of people in past societies • circumstances which governed motives and actions of people in particular societies and situations • historical significance - why societies, people and events are thought to be of historical significance.

Table 2.1: Content and Contexts of Studies[13]

develop: Is there adequate attention to Scottish/local contexts? How might you adjust topics/studies to take better account of 'studying people, events, and societies of significance in the past? What opportunities are offered in topic/studies currently taught to involve pupils in considering the meaning of heritage? Do you feel there is appropriate coverage of this key feature?'[14]

Exemplification of the other key features is particularly constructive for primary teachers, offering insight into what children should learn about the past and 'appropriate activities' to develop such learning. In discussion about 'developing an understanding of change and continuity, cause and effect', History is identified as a dynamic subject, a live issue for today's society. Children can recognise these concepts as features in their own lives and should progressively revisit them in different contexts. Without this conceptual focus, 'History would be simply a descriptive catalogue to be accepted without question'.[15] Useful pointers of advice on how a teacher could develop such concepts include: the value of a comparative study of past and present; choosing studies which show significant changes within the period; using 'line of development' studies to demonstrate change, cause and effect; choosing appropriate contexts to aid understanding of 'simple' or 'more complex' change/continuity issues. For each of the primary stages, there is helpful elaboration of the key features with a useful range of ideas for activities which go some way towards identifying not just what children should be learning about the past but how they can learn and how a progression in such learning can be developed.

Teachers often express concern about the most effective way of developing a sense of time, particularly with young children. The exemplification document makes it clear that acquiring a sense of time involves pupils in developing two particular skills, namely to describe the past 'in words or through numbers' and place people, events, artefacts and developments in sequence. It emphasises that a sense of time 'has to be consciously taught and developed', and illustrates in fair detail for each stage what children should learn and what activities would be appropriate vehicles for effective learning.[16] A clear framework for progression can be traced through which, for example, pupils will be able:

(a) using a series of simple statements, arranged in order, to describe the pupils' life or life of some other person . . . (Primary 1 – Primary 3);

(b) in listening to a story, to spot all the 'How do I know it is not now?' clues (Primary 1 – Primary 3);

(c) to build up a time-line showing key dates, century numbering, events, etc. (Primary 4 – Primary 6);

(d) to develop a retrograph (a counting backwards time-line) (Primary 4 – Primary 6);

(e) to develop and explain a time-line which spans the AD/BC divide . . . or relates to the sequencing of all topics previously studied. (Primary 7 – Secondary 2).[17]

Clearly there is no prescriptive chronological approach. Pupils can follow a programme of studies through which they move back and forth in time but teachers must have in place a framework of activities which regularly exercise their pupils' ability to describe the timescale of a particular study and locate events or studies in a historical sequence.

Hilary Cooper, among others, cites three strands to historical thinking: tracing changes over time; seeking causes and establishing effects; making deductions and inferences about sources; constructing accounts of times past.[18] The exemplification document identifies far more clearly than the initial guidelines that the focus of 'developing an understanding of the nature of historical evidence' is the development of the pupils' critical thinking through interpreting and evaluating a range of different types of sources. There is clarification for the non-specialist on sources and source handling skills, notably the questions which pupils should be encouraged to consider and ask, alongside exemplars of a range of activities which would enable pupils to scrutinise, interpret and evaluate historical evidence.[19]

Obviously such exemplification still leaves some hard decisions to be taken by teachers but it does contribute, nevertheless, to an understanding not just of what to teach but what pupils should learn and how they can learn about the past. Keith Crawford, in analysing publicised weaknesses in planning and teaching primary History in the National Curriculum, is convinced that the two key questions which primary teachers should ask themselves are, What do/should children learn about History? and How should they learn?[20] Crawford's reflections based upon OFSTED inspections show that teachers have difficulties in forging links between 'what' pupils should learn and 'why' and 'how'. The exemplification of 'Understanding People in the Past' makes it clear that studying the past for primary pupils means both acquiring a body of knowledge and a mode of enquiry which should enable them to acquire such knowledge in a genuinely historical way. In providing suggestions of 'appropriate learning activities' it helps teachers to make this crucial relationship between learning 'what' and learning 'how'. The HMI inspections of a selection of primaries across Scotland indicate that, generally, primary teachers are successful in their teaching of History, being more focused upon what pupils should be learning about the past and more effective in enabling them to do so.

The strands common to all outcomes of Environmental Studies 5–14 describe an enquiry-based process of learning which is compatible with historical enquiry. In describing the purpose of History in the school curriculum, the Scottish History Review Group highlighted certain key skills which History education sets out to develop in young people.[21] Such skills correspond well with the strands, particularly with interpreting and evaluating. From the guidance provided regarding ways of learning about the past and from interpretation of the strands, primary schools should recognise that through a programme of studies of the past pupils will develop their abilities to:

(a) ask questions, seek out appropriate sources, organise an enquiry (Planning);
(b) gather evidence from a variety of sources and use appropriate ways to collect evidence (Collecting Evidence);
(c) record evidence in a variety of ways and communicate effectively (Recording and Presenting);
(d) distinguish fact and fiction, be critical of opinion, bias and authorship, draw conclusions with justification (Interpreting and Evaluating).

This emphasis on interpreting and evaluating demonstrates the critical thinking required to construct an account of the past and mirrors the dynamic potential of historical studies as 'History is re-written as new evidence is discovered'.[22] This is also a particularly effective way in which primary teachers can fulfil an obligation placed upon them by the guidelines and help their pupils to recognise History as a subject in that 'as they progress it is important that they begin to recognise that there are different ways or modes of looking at the world and of organising human knowledge'.[23] The strands within Environmental Studies 5–14 have helped Primary schools develop key aspects of historical enquiry which should carry on into the first two years of Secondary school. However, as Duncan Toms notes in Chapter 3, the position in Secondary 1 and 2 is more problematic, not least because dropping the investigative element for Standard Grade has weakened progression from 5–14 to Secondary 3 and Secondary 4. History education requires a more comprehensive review than the current re-evaluation of Environmental Studies 5–14 to ensure a coherent and progressive programme from Primary 1 to Secondary 6.

Like so many official documents, both the guidelines and their exemplification offer no discussion and only sparse and very general advice on which attitudes historical studies could 'develop and inform'. This is particularly unfortunate when attitudes towards the past obviously matter and should be a very significant goal in teaching about the past. The guidelines provide some general statements concerning heritage, responsibility towards preservation, and developing a sense of stewardship.

However, some additional attitudes particularly pertinent to people studies could have been highlighted. For example:

(a) an ability to empathise with other people in different times and circumstances;
(b) a willingness to consider other people's values and points of view;
(c) respect and tolerance for other cultures;
(d) a rational pride in national achievements coupled with the recognition that some debt may be due to others;
(e) a disposition to enquire and question;
(f) an appreciation of their own contribution to constructing the past.

Real consideration of such attitudes at the planning stage could sharpen the aims of any historical study and enhance the understanding and interests of pupils.

Essentially, the crucial question for primary teachers is *How do you translate History as a discipline into good classroom History?* In *History 7–11*, Jon Nicol asserts that the quality of classroom History is based upon the primary teacher's grasp of three types of knowledge: substantive; syntactic and pedagogical.[24] What History is about, what can be studied, and how, is the substantive knowledge which colours the teacher's perception of what content to teach. Syntactic knowledge is the degree of understanding of the process through which historians work to learn about the past. Pedagogical knowledge is the repertoire of strategies and techniques which shapes content and processes knowledge into teaching patterns and turns academic History into studies of the past appropriate for young pupils. Even with exemplification some primary teachers, as generalists, could feel more secure with more debate and direction on the substantive dimension in terms of selecting contexts and interpreting key features and attitudes within specific studies.

The Primary Experience

When we reflect that 'Understanding People in the Past' may be the only formal History education many pupils will ever receive and that seven out of the nine years of this 5–14 experience are based in the primary classroom, then it is vital that historical studies should excite and appeal to pupils aged 5 to 12. 'To be truly effective, History education in schools must capture young people's imagination and stimulate their intellect' and a wide selection of studies should provide excellent contexts for developing both.[25]

History, after all, is essentially about people, about their actions, motives, values and lifestyles, and people are invariably intriguing. Hilary Cooper, writing about 3 to 7 year olds' abilities to learn about the past, confirms that, 'of course, chronology and dates and measured time are central to History as a discipline but for young children whose understanding of time is embryonic, a curiosity and excitement about other people, other lives and other times are more important than dates'.[26] Right from the start then, effective experiences must harness this excitement and curiosity and use them to whet and sustain such interest and develop an understanding of the past. History obviously has always had its successes with the young, in part at least. George Mackay Brown, reminiscing about his education in the Scottish system of the 1930s found his imagination, if not his intellect, whetted by his historical studies:

> History was the only subject in school that made the blood sing along my veins, but it was the romantic spindrift of History, not the great surges of tribes and economics and ideas that are the stuff of History. But I am grateful for what we got; it nourished the imagination.[27]

But the 'stuff' of History is important too and in the primary years the ways by which pupils acquire insight into and knowledge of the past are crucial if they are to build up a useful map of the past and feel positively towards History. The enquiry-based approach, sketched out in the strands and exemplification, certainly has far greater potential to stimulate the intellect than the transmission of dates, lists of kings and chronicles of events and battles experienced by the many who were never 'turned on' by History.

For primary pupils, learning about the past should involve them actively in 'doing History', in making sense of the past as historians would. As such, it should be a lively problem-solving process, developing not just a set of specific skills but understanding, attitudes and dispositions which lead to critical thinking and evaluative judgements. It is also a constructivist process of learning in that the pupils can pose their own questions based upon their experiences, feelings and personal lifestyles and reconstruct their own versions of what it could have been like to live 'then'. When 'historical knowledge, content, is the outcome of a process of enquiry that we call "doing History" ',[28] then both imagination and intellect are undoubtedly engaged and challenged.

This process of doing History depends upon the teacher's skills in handling investigations and using strategies which ensure a sound interpretation of the historical content of any study. In *History as a Construct,* Nicol and Dean refer to Hexter's theory that historians work with 'first' and 'second' records. 'First record' is made up of the original sources which have survived in any period. It is the 'second record' which is really vital because it is the understanding, experiences and perceptions which pupils require to bring to a study of the past. Nicol and Dean argue that while young pupils do have their own 'second records', they are under-developed and an enthusiastic teacher plays a central role in extending their historical thinking through skilful questioning and open discussion.[29]

The wide curricular experiences of primary teachers contribute to their considerable skills in devising and presenting activities in motivating and discerning ways. The variety of approaches which they can employ is a major catalyst in translating academic History into a dynamic and exciting classroom subject. Despite a demanding and somewhat congested curriculum, the primary teacher also has the advantage of continuous contact with his/her pupils and hence a flexibility, if required, to extend their historical insight through music, art, drama, language or even mathematics!

Primary programmes of past studies intentionally employ a wide range of approaches, selected to be appropriate to the specific content of the study and the active development of the pupils' historical thinking. Some initially use the personal History approach focusing upon the child's 'story' and that of family and friends, using photographs, toys, artefacts and living memories to develop the vocabulary of time and time-line sequence. In all programmes, the local environment is a particularly rich context for past studies with its potential for investigative visits to sites and museums and for acquiring stimulating human and documented sources of evidence which present children with real life possibilities as to how things were then and now. History brings a unique interpretation to a Place, Time and Society study of a school's environment, providing excellent opportunities for empathising with people long ago and a recurring yardstick for comparison with any societies studied elsewhere in Scotland or beyond. Often, too, History makes pupils notice things they have missed which is particularly important when it is the pupils' home territory.

Stories are a particularly effective approach to use with young pupils. Young children not only enjoy listening to stories about times, places and people outwith their experiences, but can be very active in interpreting and using their imagination to construct developments in stories. Myths, legends and folk tales go further than stories in that they look outwards at a range of societies with contrasting values and illustrate concepts, such as courage, social order, power or colonisation, which are fundamental to many societies. As such they are rich sources of study for an ancient civilisation, particularly at the Primary 6/Primary 7 stage.

Archaeology is another stimulating approach to the past. It is not only the best approach to investigate the lives of people in pre-History but an approach which sheds light on the unrecorded lives of ordinary people and their living conditions from Skara Brae to the Industrial Revolution and the Second World War.[30] It has a particular attraction for young people in that its evidence can be handled to see how it works and the skills of the archaeologist are precisely those which engage the imagination. Museum workshops have become very exciting, encouraging pupils to appreciate the value of old things and the design of early technologies. Visits to 'digs' or working with a 'simulated dig' and the creation of a time capsule of the way we live are other stimulating versions of this approach. Making deductions about people from their artefacts and creating class museums are effective ways of introducing younger children to 'then and now' and extending older pupils' insights and interpretations of Victorians or World War I.

For obvious reasons, using visual sources is a very popular approach in the primary classroom but the complexity of the images presented requires to be appreciated. Paintings of portraits, landscapes, townscapes, people at work, on the move or at leisure, even still life paintings, are useful historical sources but they were often a contrived view showing a person or society in its best light. Similarly book illustrations and photographs are interesting sources and the interaction of a CD-ROM or the raciness of a television presentation provide their own unique impact. Taking photographs on the spot in the street and discussing what people in 50 or 100 years' time might deduce from them is a useful way of showing how the children themselves can create documents of the past. Written sources can sometimes produce difficulties for primary pupils in terms of language, script, density or formality but the variety of such evidence can provide enjoyable and profitable opportunities to reflect upon how people lived and what they valued.

Oral History can be a particularly appropriate and fruitful approach for primary pupils enabling them to interact with older generations who saw and lived through changes over time in their own community, providing graphic and sometimes conflicting views on how things used to be! Usually this approach involves interviewing, in which the teacher creates a situation which will ensure some success and structures a debriefing which will look critically at the evidence gathered. Sue Cox describes an alternative approach where Year 6 pupils, through visits to identify and chart changes to their physical environment since the 1930s and through the recollections, photos, actions and feelings of a group of older residents, tried to reach a consensus on 'What was it really like?', not by interviewing but by raising questions, hypothesising, looking for clues and testing ideas. It was a constructivist approach which made them challenge their own assumptions, raise questions about What is History? and reflect on their own role in piecing together this particular story of the past.[31]

All of these approaches involve children in finding out about the past through genuine historical enquiry. Mention has already been made of the injunction upon primary teachers to ensure that their pupils should begin to recognise History as a distinctive way of looking at people, events and places. Sue Cox felt that the responses of the Year 6 pupils in the Oral History Project indicated that they were on the threshold of handling some sophisticated and complex ideas about History and they were still in Primary School. Perhaps this was an exceptional experience, but teachers can take the opportunities which arise in every study to discuss why historians work in this way and why imagination is needed to construct the story of the past.

Programmes of Studies of the Past

The 5–14 guidelines stress that programmes of studies are of crucial importance and must have a rationale and structure which ensure a balanced and progressive development of every pupil's map of the past:

> These pupils who do not continue their formal study of History . . . beyond Secondary 2 should, as a result of following a clear and coherent programme of History teaching from early Primary to Secondary 2, have established a substantial framework of historical skills and understanding which will remain with them into adult life'.[32]

Mention has already been made of the fact that the guidelines and their exemplification remain steadfast in leaving the design of programmes and choice of studies to the professional in the classroom. Hence, probably one of the most contentious issues about History education in the 5–14 curriculum, in the primary years in particular, relates to choice of contexts and content for programmes of studies. Given a very limited time allocation for History within the Environmental Studies curriculum area, teachers have to be very selective of topics and very focused on the key features of Understanding People in the Past. Reluctantly for many, cherished episodes or elements have to go while, perhaps, some new studies, appropriate to the principles of their overall rationale, have to be researched, resourced and planned.

It is reasonably straightforward for school staffs to establish the general principles for a selection of studies which will comprise a balanced and progressive programme. Some are very explicit in the guidelines. For example, studies should be selected in relation to the five prescribed eras; the pupils' own locality; Scottish, British, European and World Contexts; developing a sense of time by locating events and tracing changes through a 'line of development'; and the need for coherence, continuity and progression. Other issues influencing selection relate, of course, to the teachers' interests and expertise, to available resources, to making full use of the local area and its field study potential, to the outcomes of interchange with Secondary and other Primaries in the local cluster, and to the time management of such studies within the Social Subjects element of the Environmental Studies curriculum.

But, specifically, which contexts and which content? remains the dilemma. While this is a refreshingly flexible professional situation, it is somewhat daunting, nonetheless, for in this content debate there are several key issues to be resolved:

(a) which studies would best illustrate a Scottish narrative?

(b) to what extent should there be a British narrative and how can studies show the contribution of Scots and other nationals abroad?

(c) should studies of the past be chronological, i.e. from Skara Brae to the 1960s? What mechanism can be built in to ensure a grasp of time if studies are not chronological?

(d) to what extent should 'personal History' feature in Primary 5 – Primary 7 and Ancient Civilisations feature in Primary 1 – Primary 3? To what ways can local History be developed from Primary 1 – Primary 7?

One particular issue is that of progression and how it can be recognised across a seven year primary programme of past studies. Overall the programme's progression could be charted in terms of:

(a) increasing knowledge of the past, of recognising and explaining change/ continuity, cause and effect;

(b) more complex historical thinking, responding to 'what if' and 'why' questions;

(c) increased understanding of human behaviour, of why people acted in certain ways;

(d) making deductions from increasingly impersonal or abstract sources;

(e) locating and sequencing events using proper time vocabulary and the standard units of months, years, decades, centuries;

(f) relating events 'here' with 'there';

(g) actively promoting a range of relevant attitudes towards the past.[33]

Hence, in a progressive sequence of studies, it is possible to revisit a topic, Ancient Rome or The Vikings, at Primary 6 and develop it in a way which is not repetitious in the memories of the pupils who studied the topic in Primary 3.

Finally, there is the all-important issue of the time allocation for History in a busy primary curriculum which now has additional priorities to further language and numeracy. A school staff, reviewing its practice in order to shape its programme, could ask, 'Is sufficient time spent on History to cover adequate content and develop historical thinking?' It is important to ensure that 'adequate' can be achieved within the circumstances and to recognise the inevitability of gaps. The exemplification of overall planning for Environmental Studies 5–14 advises a strategy of balancing main topics which are studied in depth, the Victorians or World War II, with minor topics which may focus on application of skills, Our Heritage Trail, or a particular element of content in The Clearances or Jacobites.

In the interests of the most effective management of time, opportunities should be taken to link History within a Place, Time and Society based study, for example, Our School or Our Community, to avoid overload and enhance the learning by providing better coherence and continuity. It is also both feasible and desirable to incorporate a History dimension, such as the French Revolution, into a geographical study of France. Across the Social Subjects generally some studies may be discretely focused on one outcome but some will encompass more. In such studies, as in the more integrated infant topics, it is obviously very important to identify the specific historical content . A flexible pattern of such strategies makes the best use of limited time and should facilitate the delivery of a programme of History education which is both progressive and coherent. Nonetheless, the questionnaire which has now initiated the current review of Environmental Studies 5–14 seems to imply that curriculum planners recognise that some measures should be taken to assist teachers with the difficult task of meeting the demands created by the 5–14 programme within a restricted time allocation.[34] History, as part of Social Subjects, receives approximately 3 – 4 per cent of time within the primary curriculum. As Ian McKellar notes in Chapter 5 other countries do allocate more time to History. Scotland should follow their example.

Conclusion

History education is a popular element of the primary curriculum. Within the Environmental Studies area it is often the first of the Social Subjects outcomes to be teased out into a progressive programme. Despite the constraints of time and some lack of specificity from the guidelines it has emerged in the 5–14 curriculum as a recognisable 'subject'. It is now much more focused upon knowledge and understanding of the past than on the cross-curricular skills which previously formed the core of many studies.

Primary Schools have come a long way in the past three years in devising progressive programmes in the Environmental Studies curriculum. It is interesting at this time to consider what impact a new Scottish Parliament may have on this curriculum and on History education in particular, since politicians often exhibit a lively interest in History! Perhaps there will at last be a prescribed 'Scottish narrative' for schools supported by a national bank of resources. It is to be hoped that such a development will not replace the importance of curriculum decisions being made in the primary classroom.

Notes

1. Environmental Studies 5–14 Guidelines, Section 1: Rationale, Scottish Office Education and Industry Department, 1993, p.1.

2. Ibid.

3. Scottish History in the Curriculum, A Statement of Position, Scottish Consultative Council on the Curriculum, 1997, p.3.

4. Environmental Studies 5–14, Section 1: Rationale, Scottish Office Education and Industry Department, 1993, p.1.

5. Scottish History in the Curriculum, A Statement of Position, Scottish Consultative Council on the Curriculum, 1997, p.8.

6. Hilary Cooper, *History in the Early Years*, (London, 1995), p.1–4.

7. Tim Williams, 'Not Equipped to Remember', *The Scotsman*, 12/11/98.

8. S. Wood and F. Payne, 'In Search of A Scottish Identity', *Education in the North, New Series*, No. 5, 1997.

9. Scottish History in the Curriculum, A Statement of Position, Scottish Consultative Council on the Curriculum, 1997, p.3–11.

10. 'An Outpouring of Books on Scottish History', *The Scotsman*, 23/6/97.

11. Environmental Studies 5–14, Exemplification, Understanding People in the Past, Scottish Consultative Council on the Curriculum, 1996.

12. Ibid., p.1.

13. Ibid., p.2–3.

14. Ibid., p.3 and p.30.

15. Ibid., p.4.

16. Ibid., p.10.

17. Ibid., p.12–17.

18. Hilary Cooper, *History in the Early Years*, p.5.

19. Environmental Studies 5–14 Exemplification, Understanding People in the Past, Scottish Consultative Council on the Curriculum, 1996, p.20–21.

20. Keith Crawford, The Teaching and Learning of Primary History', *Teaching History*, Vol. 90, February, 1998.

21. Scottish History in the Curriculum, A Statement of Position, Scottish Consultative Council on the Curriculum, 1997, p.3–5.

22. Hilary Cooper, *History in the Early Years*, p.48.

23. Environmental Studies 5–14 Guidelines, Scottish Office Education and Industry Department, 1993, p.2.

24. J. Nicol and J. Dean, *History 7–11*, (Routledge, 1997), p.1–4.

25. Scottish History in the Curriculum, A Statement of Position, Scottish Consultative Council on the Curriculum, 1997, p.4.

26. Hilary Cooper, *History in the Early Years*, p.16.

27. George MacKay Brown, *For the Islands I Sing*, (Edinburgh, 1997), p.31.

28. J. Nicol and J. Dean, *History 7–11*, p.8.

29. Ibid., p.8–10.

30. N. Curtis, 'Archaeology for Primary School Pupils: Learning with Objects in a University Museum', *Education in the North, New Series*, No.5, 1997.

31. Sue Cox, 'Oral History: Primary Children and Older People Working Together', *Education 3–13*, March, 1998.

32. Achieving Success in Secondary 1 and Secondary 2, Scottish Office Education and Industry Department, 1996, p.14.

33. Hilary Cooper, *History in the Early Years*, p.109–119.

34. Review of Environmental Studies 5–14: Consultative Questionnaire, Scottish Consultative Council on the Curriculum, October – December, 1998.

3

History Education in Secondary Schools

Duncan Toms

When to the sessions of sweet silent thought
I summon up remembrance of things past.
(Shakespeare, Sonnet XXX)

History is a nightmare from which I am trying to awake
(James Joyce, Ulysses)

Society's Expectations

History has always been a difficult subject to pin down, not only in terms of content and causation, but also in relation to why we study it and what role it should play in our schools. In one sense it is the most practical of subjects in that in any field of life and endeavour, without an understanding of what has come before, it is impossible to understand where you are at present and to orientate yourself towards the future. At the same time, due to its vast and ever-increasing scale, we have to be ruthlessly selective in what we study, which contains the inherent danger of distortion and one-sidedness. This applies at both the individual and social levels, nationally as well as internationally. In addition, its relative lack of any immediate practical application can lead to a dangerous belief that it is an educational luxury which can be downgraded or even dispensed with, leading historians in their turn to defend it as the most important and essential of subjects.

Thus claims are made for the usefulness of History both in Scotland and further afield in terms of:

(a) national consciousness and nation building;
(b) nurturing social and civic awareness;
(c) encouraging a pluralist, democratic, tolerant outlook;
(d) developing intellectual and forensic skills of objectivity and debate;
(e) contributing to self-awareness and a sense of identity.

In the 19th and first half of the 20th centuries the first two objectives tended to be emphasised at the official political and educational levels,

34

reflecting the perceived needs of the British Empire and a developing democracy.[1] But over the past half century it is the second two which have come to be given more prominence in official literature, largely as a result of the maturation of democracy and the awful lessons of totalitarian regimes. These views are reflected, for example, in the sections on 'Rationale' at the beginning of the official Arrangements documents for teaching History to 14–16 year olds (Standard Grade)[2] and, more recently, in the Higher Still History proposals for Secondary 5 and 6 (16–18 year olds).[3]

In recent years, however, the picture has become rather more complicated with the establishment of more political autonomy or independence for nations which, for different reasons, had become partially 'submerged' either by colonisation or by incorporation into larger states. Thus in Scotland we have the debate over the importance of the teaching of Scottish History which, if not carefully handled, given the limited time available for teaching History as a whole, could come into conflict with the development of wider intellectual skills and humanist values. Such developments, particularly in eastern Europe, have been one of the main motivating factors in the formation of EUROCLIO (the European Standing Conference of History Teachers' Associations) and European-wide co-operation in History teaching.

One of the features of History teaching in Scotland, as in England, Wales and Northern Ireland, is that, unlike many other countries, the subject is not compulsory after the age of 14 and is continued thereafter by a minority of students. Since History is always grouped with the other 'social subjects' (Geography and Modern Studies), however, it seems likely that any move towards making the subject compulsory post-14 would result in a watered-down 'integrated' social subjects course with less time for History as such for those specifically interested in it. The experience of such 'integrated' courses further down the school is not a happy one and any gains in terms of numbers could well be lost in terms of student motivation. Such ill-conceived attempts to 'rationalise' the social subjects may well increase if 'millennium' proposals to replace subject department principals with 'faculty' (social subjects?) heads are proceeded with. Nor is this just a selfish practical consideration from the teacher's point of view. The compulsory teaching of Mathematics post-14, probably has the effect of putting the majority of people off the subject for life. If the subject was made optional post-14 it would enable more pupils to opt for other subjects. This is not such an outrageous suggestion when one considers that the majority of people use only the most basic arithmetic after they have left school whereas History and other social subjects become, if anything, even more relevant in later life.

In some countries where History is compulsory post-14, its main function seems to be the inculcation of a national, even nationalist, body of knowledge and set of values. Although official examination arrangements for Standard

Grade,[4] Higher and Sixth Year Studies[5] mean that the content of History teaching post-14 is restricted to a fairly limited range of options, Scotland has escaped the rigidities of a national syllabus or curriculum – particularly in the 5–14 age range. The positive side of this is that it makes political manipulation and over-concentration on particular topics difficult and leaves room for individual strengths and interests. The down-side is that it can lead to the relative neglect of History in some Primary Schools and makes the centralised production of support materials difficult especially for commercial publishers.

But, when all is said and done, the official reasons for the teaching of History in schools may be the reasons why politicians attach more or less importance to it and invest more or less money in it but below that stratospheric level we all have our own reasons. For most educational officials and managers from the Scottish Office and Inspectorate, through local authority administrators, down to the headteachers and school management teams, History is a relatively minor mountain in the educational landscape (or slot(s) in the time-table) to be more or less tolerated 'because it is there'. And, judging by the fact that the majority of them give the subject up at the first opportunity, most pupils from 5–14 are 'doing' it because they are conscripts with no choice in the matter – which is not to say that they do not find it useful and interesting up to a point. Which leaves us with the History teachers themselves and their select band of more or less enthusiastic volunteers ('it's not as bad as Geography and Modern Studies') aged 14–18. Why do they choose to study History? Since they are in a sense the grain of sand round which the pearl of historical understanding forms in the oyster of society (only to be cast before the swine?), an analysis of what motivates them could provide the key to the further encouragement and development of History both in schools and further afield.

Individual Motivation

Like teachers of other subjects, most History teachers have probably ended up in History teaching largely as a result of having liked and been good at the subject at school themselves. They can, therefore, be seen as highly evolved specimens of those students who choose to stay with History post-14. So why then does History appeal more to some pupils than to others? The answer(s) to this question should provide some insight into History's continuing place in society. Nor should we see the issue through rose-tinted spectacles and ignore the fact that some of the most malign individuals over the centuries have had a powerful sense of History. In a notorious passage in *Mein Kampf*, for example, Hitler extolled the virtues of his school History teacher in surprisingly modern terms.[6]

The History department in my school (Bearsden Academy) recently carried out a survey of Secondary 2 pupils (aged 14) who had just made their subject choice prior to going into Standard Grade courses in Secondary 3. The first question listed a number of possible reasons for choosing History of which pupils could tick as many as they felt applied. The results were as follows:

Reason	Girls (%)	Boys (%)	Total (%)
Marks/grades	81	59	72
The topics	61	68	64
Work/activities	52	41	47
The teacher	13	23	17
Parental advice	32	27	30
Guidance advice	16	4	11
Friend(s) choice	0	4	2

Table 3.1: Reasons for Choosing History

In addition 17 per cent indicated 'enjoyment' in a section for 'any other reasons' and a similar number put 'career requirements'. Most of the latter were girls, probably suggesting a more conscientious/enthusiastic/helpful attitude to filling out questionnaires, and indicating a weakness in the original list of options. If these two additional reasons had been included in the list more might have been prompted to choose them.

The overall results are not all that surprising in that success appears to be the main motivator – it is easier to enjoy a subject if you are relatively good at it – and teachers, whether subject or guidance, do not feature particularly high on the list, being well out-stripped by parental influence on choice. Apart from that it is the gender differences which are most striking with the girls' choice tending to be more influenced by marks, work and guidance and the boys by the topics and the teacher.

The main point of the questionnaire, however, was to find out why more pupils were not choosing History so that we could do something about it . Here the results were as follows:

Reason	Girls (%)	Boys (%)	Total (%)
Marks/grades	32	38	34
The topics	41	41	41
Work/activities	36	51	43
The teacher	20	23	21
Parental advice	16	35	24
Guidance advice	9	18	13
Friend(s) choice	0.5	0.5	1

Table 3.2: Reasons for Not Choosing History

Here lack of interest in the work and topics seems to be the main demotivator rather than the marks achieved. Other interesting contrasts with Table 3.1 are the positive influence of parental and guidance advice on girls whereas for boys they appear to have a negative effect, even if the overall figures are comparable.

The middle section of the questionnaire attempted to identify which particular aspects of the History course (in terms of topics and work activities) pupils found more or less interesting and enjoyable with a view to modifying the course to make it more attractive. The results of this section are too detailed and specific to reproduce here but they also revealed some interesting gender differences. The political and military History of the Second World War was generally popular with all categories (girls and boys, historians and non-historians) but the Home Front held less appeal for the boys. Similarly the Scottish/British 1500–1750 topics were more popular with the girls than the boys.

The last section attempted to find out pupils' relative perceptions of the subject in relation to the other social subjects. The results were as follows:

Subject	Most Interesting (%)	Most Useful (%)	Hardest (%)
History	30	14	55
Geography	29	42	39
Modern Studies	55	57	17

Table 3.3: Pupils' Relative Perceptions of the Social Subjects
(columns total more than 100 per cent as some pupils chose joint firsts)

So, at least in my school, the tasks seem to be: to do topics/activities which interest the pupils more, to step up the propaganda on the usefulness and relevance of History, and to make the work/tests a bit easier.

The Curricular Framework

But to what extent are History teachers and their pupils encouraged or inhibited by the curricular framework within which they have to operate at different stages? Apart from the headteacher and school management team of deputy and assistant heads, there are a number of official agencies producing directives and/or guidelines for controlling and/or assisting the teaching of History. At the top of the Scottish educational pyramid are Her Majesty's Inspectors (HMI – made up of sector and subject specialists) in the Scottish Office Education and Industry Department (SOEID) currently answerable to the Secretary of State for Scotland and the minister with responsibility for Education at the Scottish Office, but soon to be answerable to their equivalents from the Scottish Parliament. Mainly ex-teachers, they are an influential presence on many educational committees and quangos, and produce information, advice and guidelines in the form of reports which are effectively directives, by virtue of the fact that they constitute the criteria according to which schools and subject departments are inspected.[7] Their power has been enhanced in recent years by the reform of local government which, by abolishing the large Regions with their educational responsibilities, led to the fragmentation and reduction of local authority educational policy making and support services. History teachers and departments are no more victimised by the Inspectorate than other subjects (the current Chief Inspector is a historian), and they seem to be regarded with rather more professional respect than their colleagues in England.

But most teachers are only concerned about the inspectors when they decide to visit their school. Of more immediate concern is the Scottish Qualifications Authority (SQA), another government appointed body, which, through its control of qualifications, exam procedures and syllabuses, determines most of what is taught in schools post-14. Hitherto it has been advised by subject panels, including one for History, consisting of a majority of classroom teachers together with representatives from the teacher training institutions, the universities, colleges, the inspectorate and an SQA official. These panels are responsible to the SQA for all matters relating to their subject, including syllabus and examinations. With the development of the unified post-16 curriculum of Higher Still, however, these panels are shortly to be replaced by a two-tier system of multi-subject advisory groups and subject assessment panels.[8] The fear is that this may leave subject specialists and classroom practitioners with a more limited input to the detriment of their respective subjects – although the increased workload required to supervise all the additional qualifications will probably be the biggest problem.

The other main government appointed body with an educational remit is the Scottish Consultative Council on the Curriculum (SCCC) – and the Scottish Council for Educational Technology (SCET) with which it looks likely to be amalgamated. The SCCC's job is to advise the government on all matters relating to the curriculum. It draws up guidelines for schools on how much time to devote to different 'modes' or groups of subjects, affectionately (?) known as 'the yellow peril' after the colour of its cover, now in the process of revision.[9] The SCCC also recently instigated reviews on the place of Scottish History and culture in the curriculum.[10] These have stirred up quite a bit of controversy or 'healthy debate' as we History teachers prefer to call a good no-holds barred punch-up. Most History teachers welcomed the opportunity to highlight the importance of Scottish History, but resented the accusation that they had been neglecting it, pointing to the many Scottish topics studied at 5–14 and the significant Scottish content of Standard Grade as well as the opportunity to study Nationalism and Devolution at Higher, but also making the point that lack of time made it impossible to cover any area of History adequately. The SCCC is now producing support materials for Scottish History in the form of a series of CD-ROMs. This is, of course, the particular area of expertise of SCET – to encourage and develop the use of such technology in teaching. There is an increasing amount of quite good software available for History at fairly reasonable prices but the problem now is to find the time to integrate it into course-work given the limited availability of hardware.

The last significant national organisation in terms of History teaching in Scotland is the purely voluntary, unofficial Scottish Association of Teachers of History (SATH). Made up of History teachers, its main functions are: to organise conferences; publish its *Resources Review* and *History Teaching Review Yearbook*; exchange ideas and assist colleagues with the classroom teaching of History; and represent the views of its members on all matters relating to History in schools. Since the drastic reduction in the number of local authority subject advisers and the decision of the main teachers' union, the Educational Institute of Scotland (EIS), to replace its subject sections with wider subject groupings, SATH has become the only national body representing the views and interests of History teachers *per se*. The increased tendency to leave teachers to their own devices, time and resources when it comes to their professional development – highlighted recently by the SQA chief's admission that Higher Still in-service training should have been directed at all secondary teachers rather than just department principals[11] – is quite scandalous, especially given the increased political/public focus on teacher competence and appraisal. But to return to the place of History itself in schools.

Secondary 1 and 2

At both primary and secondary the main constraint is the very limited time available for teaching History. This is particularly meagre in the first two years of secondary with most pupils getting less than an hour a week over the course of the year or 3 hours a week for a third of the year, i.e. not much more than 30 hours. This makes it impossible to fulfil society's expectations of imparting an adequate core or outline of historical knowledge or, as the recent SCCC Report on Scottish History in the Curriculum put it, 'a map of the past'.[12] Hence the recurring criticisms of History in schools as not doing enough Scottish History – hardly surprising in view of the fact that there is not enough time to do justice to any kind of History. In fact, if any area of History is relatively neglected, it is non-European World History.

The situation in primary is no better. Although a primary teacher with a particular interest in History can find more time for the subject by incorporating elements of it into other work, constant, often ill-informed, political and public comment on the so-called 'basics' (reading, writing and arithmetic) mean that over the country as a whole History is not given a very high priority within the overall Primary curriculum.

The 5–14 Report on Environmental Studies[13] made a commendable attempt to find a way through these severe restrictions, not by imposing further restrictions in the form of a national curriculum as in England, but by drawing up very broad guidelines for 'understanding people in the past' in the form of 'key features' to be addressed. The aim was to ensure that, even if young people's knowledge of History was bound to be inadequate given the very limited time available, it would at least be balanced. Six broad aims were identified:

(1) studying people, events and societies of significance in the past;
(2) developing an understanding of change and continuity, cause and effect;
(3) developing an understanding of time and historical sequence;
(4) developing an understanding of the nature of historical evidence;
(5) considering the meaning of heritage;
(6) learning, understanding and using appropriate language, terminology and symbols.[14]

In terms of content, pupils in Primary 1 – Primary 3 should focus on the past in terms of themselves, their families, their local environment and stories. From Primary 4 to Secondary 2 there was no detailed prescription of content but over the course of those six years studies should:

(a) be drawn from the following five periods:
  1) the Ancient World (pre fifth-century);
  2) the Middle Ages (400–1450);
  3) Renaissance, Reformation and the Age of Discovery (1450–1700);
  4) The Age of Revolutions (1700–1900);
  5) The Twentieth Century.
(b) include Scottish contexts and at least one British, one European and one non-European context;
(c) trace particular developments across time, for example, farming, transport, housing;
(d) include reference to important events and contributions of individuals;
(e) show how past events have had significant effects on present societies;
(f) include, in Primary 7–Secondary 2, political, economic, social and cultural aspects of History.[15]

This has left teachers a lot of freedom to develop courses with considerable local variations and taking advantage of their own areas of strength, and made political manipulation by central or local government (but not by individual teachers) very difficult. But there has been a price to pay. Firstly, the wide variety of topics and the variations in approach and coverage of the same topics, has made the central and/or commercial production of good quality text-books and support materials very difficult. Secondly, proper implementation of the guidelines requires a degree of Primary-Secondary liaison which has not generally proved feasible, partly because the teachers have not been given the time to do it and partly because, as a result of parental freedom of choice of schools, many secondaries have pupils from a fairly large number of primaries with considerable variations in their study of History. This has led recently to pressure for a more defined History syllabus for 5–14 particularly in relation to Scottish History. If we are pushed more in that direction, it is to be hoped that we will avoid the worst excesses of the over-prescribed national curriculum in England – perhaps by a fairly flexible menu of content options – and not go for Scottocentrism any more than Anglo, Britto or Eurocentrism. It should also be used not simply to place further restrictions on teachers and pupils but to raise History's profile and importance. This was meant to be the advantage of the national History syllabus in England but already the subject is being downgraded there.

The 5–14 programme generally also ran into difficulties in relation to assessment. In the social subjects six 'strands' or skills are meant to be assessed over five levels of ability or performance (A–E)[16] with the relatively recent addition of a sixth level F. The 'strands' are: knowledge and understanding; planning; collecting evidence; recording and presenting; interpreting and evaluating; and developing informed attitudes. Unfortunately many of the detailed 'targets', while generally worthwhile objectives in terms of teaching and learning, are not readily distinguishable, or sometimes even understandable, in terms of assessment. And, in view of the fact that the assessment proposals were very different from practice at the time, failure to produce exemplar test items was also a serious weakness. The whole issue was further complicated by the political spectre of 'national testing' and the suspicion that it would be used, not as an educational tool, but as a device for selecting pupils by ability and as a weapon for beating teachers and schools. All these factors have contributed to the recent decision to redraft the 5–14 Environmental Studies guidelines with more defined content and simplified assessment. Whether any good will come of it remains to be seen, but it is ironic that, at the same time as 5–14 assessment is being simplified, post-16 assessment is being amplified and made more onerous on both students and teachers under the Higher Still proposals – although other aspects of the History Arrangements have been generally well received.

Standard Grade (14–16)

The development of Higher Still qualifications for the large number of pupils who stay on at school post-16 has also placed a question mark over the future of Standard Grade courses and exams which were developed in the 1980s as a replacement for 'O' grades which, like the current Higher, catered only for the more academic. In History, as well as developing courses and exams for almost all levels of ability, the development of Standard Grade was also used as an opportunity to replace the primarily content-based courses and exams with a more skills-based approach reflecting the emergence of the so-called 'new History' in the 1970s. Thus evaluating historical sources and investigating historical issues were given equal weighting with knowledge and understanding in terms of course assessment outcomes. Despite good intentions, the somewhat formulaic approach to assessment adopted, combined with the volume of content to be covered (in about 160 minutes a week), has not generally had the effect of freeing up classroom teaching to allow for a more flexible activities-based approach (further exacerbated in quite a few instances by class sizes of up to 30). Recently the difficulties associated with the internal teacher assessment of the pupils' individual investigations in the social subjects led to investigating being combined with source evaluation to constitute a new 'Enquiry Skills' component in the external exam,[17] whereas most History teachers were in favour of a continuation of the individual investigation in some form but with a controlled write-up period (to minimise unfair practices) and external assessment (to render it more uniform and credible) along the lines of the prepared or 'extended' essay at Higher which has proved very successful.[18]

In terms of content pupils study three Units over the two years with each unit consisting of a number of optional contexts:[19]

Unit I: Changing Life in Scotland and Britain (social, economic, political change)
    Context A: 1750s–1850s
    Context B: 1830s–1930s
    Context C: 1880s–1980s

Unit II: International Co-operation and Conflict
    Context A: 1790s–1820s (French/Napoleonic Wars and Congress System)
    Context B: 1890s–1920s (First World War and League of Nations)
    Context C: 1930–1960s (Second World War and Cold War)

Unit III: People and Power
    Context A: USA 1850– 1880
    Context B: India 1917–1947

Context C: Russia 1914–1941
Context D: Germany 1918–1939

Most schools do Context B or C in Unit I with a few doing Context A. This is largely because when the course was first introduced there were no support materials for Context A. This is a pity because the period 1750–1850 contains many of the key turning points and developments of the past 250 years and provides more dramatic contrasts with the present day. It also contains more scope for Scottish contextualisation and provides useful background for the modern British option (1850–1979) which most pupils study at Higher anyway. In Unit II, Context B on the First World War is by far and away the most popular, with a few doing Context C and practically no-one doing Context A. This is largely because the First World War was a popular topic under the old 'O' grade and most schools were well resourced for it – together with the fact that quite a large number of schools do the Second World War both at Primary and in Secondary 1 and 2. In Unit III Russia and Germany are the most popular topics with a few doing the USA and hardly anyone doing India. This is partly because very little, if any, support materials were produced for the last two topics. Like the First World War, Russia was a popular and well resourced option at 'O' grade. There has been some criticism of the inclusion of Germany 1918–1939, however, as it is also a popular topic in Secondary 2, Higher and Certificate of Sixth Year Studies (CSYS), and there is quite a widespread feeling that it is being overdone at the expense of other possible topics.

Higher and Higher Still (16+)

After Standard Grade an even smaller number of pupils opt to continue with History. Hitherto those achieving Credit at History Standard Grade have gone on to do the subject at Higher (with 200–300 minutes a week class time). History also has a very good record for General pupils passing the Higher, while Foundation pupils could opt for a variety of Scottish Vocational Education Council (SCOTVEC) modules. All these courses are about to be superseded by new modularised Higher Still courses at 3 levels – Higher, Intermediate 2 and Intermediate 1 with Access courses below that level.[20] The outcomes and performance criteria for these courses build to varying degrees on the knowledge and understanding and enquiry skills (source evaluation and research tasks) previously developed at Standard Grade. The content of the Intermediate modules has been brought into line with the current Higher options which are to continue more or less unchanged (apart from the inclusion of a new option on Scottish popular culture, 1880–1939[21]). This is intended to ease problems of resourcing and bi-level classes. Thus at

Higher teachers can choose three units from either medieval, early modern or modern History, including one Scottish/British unit, one European/world unit and one special topic for source based work and assessment. Most schools do the modern period specifically the options on: Britain 1850–1979; Germany 1815–1939; and Appeasement and the Road to War to 1939. The first two units are assessed by an essay question paper and the special topic by a source-based question paper.

At Intermediate, History departments will be able to pick and mix three units from any period as long as there is at least one Scottish/British unit and one European/world unit. In practice, unless they have a discrete Intermediate section, they will be somewhat constrained by the need to co-ordinate it with their Higher course. Intermediate assessment will be similar in appearance to that at Standard Grade with source-based questions testing knowledge and understanding and evaluating, supplemented at Intermediate 2 by some questions, including a short essay, based purely on recall. In addition, at both Higher and Intermediate 2, candidates have to undertake a prepared 'extended essay' or 'response' on an issue of their own choosing from the course units studied. This is externally assessed by the SQA and contributes towards the overall award.

Those who do well at Intermediate 2 can go on to do the Higher in 6th year while a small number of those passing Higher will go on to do the Advanced Higher (formerly Certificate of Sixth Year Studies). The latter is highly valued by most History teachers and University History Departments in Scotland. It consists of 13 options from pre-History to the 20th century and includes Scottish, British, European, Asian, African and American topics. Schools or, in some cases, the candidates themselves choose one option for in-depth study and are assessed through essay and source-based question papers together with a 4,000-word dissertation on a course-related topic of their own choosing. Unfortunately, despite being generally acknowledged as a most rewarding course and an excellent preparation for the self-disciplined study required at university, school and university managements have hitherto generally failed to appreciate its worth with the former putting it low (last?) on their priorities for time-tabling and the latter reluctant to accord it added value as an entrance qualification. This in turn discourages pupils from doing it and the resultant small numbers cause school managements to give it even less consideration. The highly unsatisfactory situation of CSYS candidates working on their own or at the back of Higher classes is likely to become worse with Higher Still due to the increased priority which will inevitably be given to Intermediate courses and sections.

But generally speaking History teachers, unlike many of their colleagues, are reasonably satisfied with the overall structure, content and support materials for the Higher Still Arrangements for History but, like teachers of other subjects, they are less than happy with the internal assessment proposals. This is not because they are against internal assessment. They have always done it week-in and week-out as an essential part of the job. Internal assessments are used to give pupils practice and advice and the results are used for the purposes of SQA estimates and appeals. But, under Higher Still, internal assessment of units by the teacher will become a formal, centrally moderated process and candidates will have to pass all three internal unit assessments before qualifying for the externally assessed course award. Like teachers of other subjects, History teachers are against this formalisation of internal assessment on a number of grounds: assessment will become a series of hurdles to be overcome rather than a series of 'pit-stops' for servicing with the teacher appearing more as an extension of the SQA rather than an adviser and helpmate; fewer pupils will qualify since, at the moment, weakness in one element of the course can be compensated for by strength in another element; the requirements of reassessment, internal appeals and central moderation will take up time for bureaucratic procedures at the expense of learning, teaching and enjoyment of the subject; the use of check-lists of performance criteria in some aspects of the proposed internal assessment procedures is formulaic, artificial and does not accord very well with the nature of how History is studied.

Nor are teachers impressed by the argument that all this palaver of formalised internal assessment is required to ensure achievement of all the outcomes, performance criteria and core skills because the latter will only be 'sampled' by a shortened external exam. Experience of internal assessment for SCOTVEC modules and Standard Grade Investigations indicates that it is not a particularly precise tool, so to depend on it for delivery of such specific objectives is a bit like putting telescopic sights on a blunderbuss or, since the aim of assessment is to shed light rather than to maim, a Verey pistol. In addition, it looks as though History will not be particularly well served in terms of the 'core skills' proposals anyway and this, together with the proposed Scottish Group Awards, could possibly affect pupil subject choices to the detriment of History and other social subjects.

Conclusion

The contumacious tone which is perhaps the historian's fate should not be allowed to obscure the fact that teaching History to 12–18 year olds (and the odd adult) in Scotland can be very rewarding, certainly challenging and even enjoyable. Like English and a small number of other subjects, History enables the teacher to engage with the pupils' own views and interests in a way which is more difficult for most other teachers who are often limited in this respect by the nature of their subjects. Thus over the past 30 years, History in schools has opened up as an arena in which to argue and debate about evidence and interpretations of the past as well as its more traditional role of perpetuating a more or less socially consensual picture of the past within the time available. Through its development of critical respect for evidence and alternative interpretations, debating techniques and other transferable skills it has come to serve individual needs as well as social functions in a much more balanced way.

Even if at times teachers feel frustrated and constrained by the demands of the educational authorities in terms of the syllabus and assessment on the one hand, and by the need to get the pupils to get on with their work on the other, such difficulties must not be our main focus or we will only suffer along with History, the subject of our love and labours. At the end of the day, we are all – teachers, pupils, authorities – on the same side and have all played a role in continuing, encouraging and developing the study of History – even if not always to the extent or in directions which each of us might want. But it is worth reiterating, as we enter the next millennium, that if History teaching is to prosper, History teachers are the key players. Only they have the motive and capacity to be the ambassadors for their subject to the authorities and society generally, on the one hand, and to be the missionaries and proselytisers of the subject to the next generation on the other. We can do this most effectively not by dwelling on our difficulties but by playing to History's many strengths.

Notes

1. R.D. Anderson, *Education and the Scottish People* 1750–1918, (Oxford, 1995), chapter 8, Making Citizens, p.193–220.

2. Standard Grade Arrangements in History, Scottish Qualifications Authority (1997), p.4–5.

3. Higher Still Development Unit, Arrangements for History, (Edinburgh, 1997), p.1–3.

4. Standard Grade Arrangements in History, Scottish Qualifications Authority, p.10–21.

5. Revised Arrangements in History Higher and CSYS, (Scottish Examination Board, 1990), p. 9–21, and p. 27–32.

6. Adolf Hitler, *Mein Kampff*, ed. D.C. Watt, (London, 1969), p.13–14.

7. For example, Effective Learning and Teaching in Secondary Schools – History, Scottish Office Education Department, 1992.

8. Scottish Qualifications Authority, A Consultation Paper on SQA Advisory Groups, (Glasgow, 1998).

9. Scottish Consultative Council on the Curriculum, Curriculum Design for the Secondary Stages, Guidelines for Schools, Consultative Draft, (Dundee, 1998).

10. Scottish Consultative Council on the Curriculum, Scottish History in the Curriculum, (Dundee, 1998).

11. David Henderson, 'Wrong call' on stalled Highers, *Times Educational Supplement Scotland*, 27.11.98.

12. Scottish Consultative Council on the Curriculum, Scottish History in the Curriculum, (Dundee, 1998), p.3.

13. Scottish Office Education Department, Environmental Studies 5–14, (Edinburgh, 1993).

14. Ibid., p.34.

15. Ibid.

16. Ibid., p.38–45.

17. Standard Grade Arrangements in History, Scottish Qualifications Authority, p. 8–9, 28.

18. Revised Arrangements in History Higher and CSYS, Scottish Examination Board, p. 22, 24.

19. Standard Grade Arrangements in History, Scottish Qualifications Authority, p. 10–21.

20. Higher Still Development Unit, Arrangements for History, (Edinburgh, 1997).

21. Higher Still Development Unit, *Changing Scottish Society 1880s–1939, Support Materials*, (Edinburgh, 1998).

4

The Examiner's Tale

Ian Matheson

The Reasons

Tests . . . assessments . . . examinations – experiences seen as threatening, even terrifying, by large numbers of people. Many are deterred from undertaking learning opportunities because of their fear of 'the exam', or more accurately by the fear that they might fail. Yet all of us are tested, assessed, examined every day of our lives by our friends, relatives, colleagues and employers. Few of these processes are in any way formal, even fewer are subject to independent scrutiny, but the results affect our lives much more deeply and certainly more immediately than any under the auspices of the Scottish Qualifications Authority. They affect our most personal relationships for good or evil, often with no recourse of appeal to independent arbiters when the result is unpleasant. Everyone accepts these processes as a normal part of living, to the extent that we are rarely aware of their taking place.

If such processes are inbuilt in every aspect of life, it is natural that assessment is an integral part of most courses of study, especially where a successful outcome leads to a recognised qualification. There is, of course, a massive demand for such qualifications. They have currency as evidence of achievement and the attainment of particular academic standards or of competence in a specific skill. Most people aspire to obtain qualifications because they offer progression to new opportunities in employment or further study. For qualifications to be of practical value, they must have currency in the eyes of employers, professional bodies, further and higher education institutions, all of whom rely on them as evidence of a candidate's suitability to take up such an opportunity.

Scotland has an enormous advantage over many other countries in that the major qualifications in non-advanced education are certificated by a single body in the Scottish Qualifications Authority. The Quality Assurance procedures of the Scottish Qualifications Authority provide a guarantee of consistency in the application of a single standard across the country, something which cannot be guaranteed where responsibility is divided among several bodies, all offering qualifications with the same title but with no independent auditor to maintain equivalence. This leads to public confidence in a common understanding of what a particular qualification means, which explains the national headlines when an occasional politician makes a barbed observation about alleged falling standards should pass rates go up. (In passing, the Scottish Qualifications Authority cannot win here. If pass rates rise, Jeremiahs conclude that the standard necessary for obtaining a pass has been allowed to fall; if they fall, the same pundits are just as certain that this is incontrovertible evidence of falling attainment! The consequence of this is that, because the Scottish Qualifications Authority and its examiners know this equation, they strive very hard to sustain the same standard from year to year and let the sound waves from the pundits crash over their heads and run into the sands of time. Please remember this, as it will become important later.)

This advantage has been recognised by the international education community, for the Scottish Qualifications Authority is now asked on a regular basis to act as a consultant to developing countries wishing to establish their own examination systems. It also receives requests from advanced countries to participate in benchmarking exercises to enable them to assess the standing of their own qualifications in international terms.

The Structure

In Scotland, the most highly regarded qualification remains the Higher Grade, shortly to be renamed Higher Level under the Higher Still reforms. Its status makes it even more essential that every effort is made to maintain consistency in the examination procedures and sustain public confidence.

In History, the new Higher Still syllabus at Higher Level will reflect very closely the revised syllabus introduced in 1991, with a few revisions as a result of identified syllabus overload or to remove areas which were failing to attract candidates. The Specialist Working Group took the decision to follow a model of minimum change because it recognised that the History teaching profession has confidence in the syllabus and examination devised by the Joint Working Group 10 years ago.

This confidence results from the principles upon which the syllabus was founded, which sought to reflect good practice in the study and teaching of History. It recognised the continuing value of extended writing as a discipline; this is, after all, a skill integral to the study of History and at the same time an ability valued in many professions. At the same time it sought to introduce an awareness of historical methods, both through practising the research skills required and through handling source evidence, primary and secondary, in the Special Topic.

Where the Joint Working Group departed from the perceptions of the cynics was in devising an examination structure which actually reflected the skills, as well as the knowledge, which the course was designed to foster.

Research skills were built into the preparation for the first real novelty, the Extended Essay, a device intended to provide students with the opportunity to demonstrate their writing skills free from at least some of the constraints which are often seen as barriers to performance: the over reliance on memorised fact and the time pressure of the formal examination. By selecting their own themes, and even their own questions, candidates are able to choose an area of the course which they find interesting and delve into it in more depth than is possible in the class routine. They have the opportunity to investigate the work of professional historians, to discover historiography and the remarkable truth that evidence can be interpreted in more than one way. They are even required to prepare an essay plan in advance, a process intended to encourage the drafting and redrafting of their ideas, to develop understanding and to enable them to consider the evidence and how it will be used to illustrate and develop an argument or debate. Then they have two hours to translate this plan into a thoughtful and literate piece of work. The innovative History teachers who devised this concept had two purposes: to allow the candidates to display their very best work and to further their training in the skills of essay writing, in the hope that it would transfer to the unseen elements of the examination. In practice, the first of these hopes has been realised to a truly impressive extent. Regrettably, there is much less evidence that the second has been achieved, no doubt due to the pressures of time and panic that tend to surround all examinations.

The second major innovation in the Revised syllabus which has been retained into Higher Still is the testing of source handling skills. The previous Alternative Higher examination had contained extracts, usually from secondary sources, but these were used solely as triggers for recall questions. In the Revised syllabus and in Higher Still candidates are presented with a mixture of primary and secondary sources which they have to use in order to answer questions which test their ability to interpret and compare the sources and to evaluate them in the light of their recalled knowledge. The task of integrating the evidence from the sources and from recall is undoubtedly the greatest challenge, but one which gives able candidates a chance to score very high marks.

To summarise, the examination contains three parts, including the Extended Essay. In Paper I, students write three essays (under Higher Still this will become two) on their chosen Option, Medieval, Early Modern or Later Modern History. Paper II assesses their ability to interpret, compare and evaluate sources and to place them in their historical context, based on the Special Topic which they have been studying. This paper has separate sections for each of the Special Topics, whose subjects range from the Crusades through Scotland 1689–1714 and the American Revolution to Appeasement, the Cold War and 20th-century Ireland.[1]

Setting the Examination – Principles and Practice

'How could they ask a question like that?'

'That paper was unfair – it missed out topics I spent two months teaching.'

'They shouldn't be allowed to miss out Bismarck/women's suffrage/the October Revolution . . . (insert your own priority topic)'

'Whoever made up that examination must have been in a bad temper/ drunk/ trying to catch us out . . . (insert your own phrase)'

Have you ever felt like that about a Higher History paper? Ever written to complain? Ever wondered if the whole thing was made up in half an hour by someone with only a passing knowledge of History?

No wonder being asked to be involved in the setting of a public national examination is a daunting prospect. Setters and examiners are aware that they carry two different, but equally important, responsibilities. First, they are the custodians of the national standards referred to above, so must endeavour to ensure that the examination papers, year by year, present as closely as possible the same challenge to candidates. At the same time, they are responsible to the candidates themselves and to the teachers who prepare them for examination, to ensure that the examination is a fair test which allows candidates to demonstrate what they *have* learned, not an attempt to find out what they have *not* learned.

Before attempting to carry out these responsibilities by setting a paper, the examiners in Higher History meet about 18 months before the examination is due to take place to agree on common principles to ensure that the papers, whether in Medieval, Early or Later Modern, are comparable in the demands they make on candidates. Among these are:

(a) reasonable sampling of syllabus content, not only within the paper concerned, but when taken in the context of preceding papers;

(b) variety in question styles and stems, in order to avoid making the papers look boring;

(c) in Paper II, agreeing on maximum and minimum word counts for the sources in each Special Topic, to make reading demands as similar as possible, taking into account the different rhythms of language in different periods of History;

(d) including, where suitable examples can be found which fit naturally into the setter's plan, a visual source in each Special Topic; and

(e) phrasing the questions as clearly as possible in order to minimise the possibility of misinterpretation.

The last of these is by far the most important to ensure a fair test. By a similar distance, it is also the most difficult to achieve, as candidates are human, therefore infinitely inventive in discovering ways of, or in some cases excuses for, reading the question they *want* to find instead of the one which is actually there. No examiner knows whether the paper (s)he has set is 'easy' or 'hard' until the candidates produce their responses. Over the years the Higher History team has learned certain lessons which it now applies rigorously. Two examples may illustrate. *No* question in a Higher History examination will now appear which begins with the word 'how' on its own; 'how far . . .', 'how important . . .' or 'how significant . . .' are fine, but not 'how did . . .'. Why? Because a large proportion of the people of Scotland (at all ages) does not distinguish between 'how' and 'why'. If someone wants to question the reason behind something you have said, you are likely to be asked 'how'?

Secondly, it is common for candidates to seek to answer a question on a particular period and to distort questions to 'justify' their desires. For example, this is apparent in questions relating to the development of democracy in Britain, and especially on women's rights. Ask any question on this topic and the candidate leaps on it as an opportunity to relate the story of the Women's Social and Political Union, particularly the campaigns inspired by Christabel Pankhurst and the gory details of forcible feeding. To limit the opportunities for examination time travelling, all questions which *might*, however remotely, be interpreted as referring to different periods now carry terminal dates to make the examiner's intention as clear as possible. Regrettably, there are still a few candidates who insist on answering the question on the Suffragettes they have prepared for, even where the question refers to '. . . between 1928 and 1979'.

So, the setter has created a draft of the sources and questions proposed for the examination. The next stage is to send these (by secure postal systems!) to the Principal Examiner (Assessor under Higher Still terminology) – that is, to me. Once I have had an opportunity to peruse the draft and, usually, prepare some suggestions for amendments, a telephone call with each setter results in an agreed draft to send to the Scottish Qualifications Authority. In general, setters tend to find this a useful exercise, for it is easy to find difficulties in phrasing questions through coming very close to the material; a second pair of eyes is often valuable in clarifying the idea behind a question.

This draft is then the focus of my meeting with three moderators appointed by the Authority, usually two Principal Teachers and a representative of the Higher Education sector. At this meeting, the draft is discussed in great detail, with two main considerations in mind. First, is the language of the sources (and the questions) appropriate for this level of examination? It is common for sources to be edited further at this stage for accessibility, perhaps by the use of full stops to create two shorter sentences, by removing pieces of text or by replacing vocabulary that is dated or over-complex. Second, is the meaning of each question sufficiently clear? Where necessary, questions are rephrased to improve clarity. This process arrives at a proposed revised draft, which is then discussed again with the setters to ensure that they feel comfortable with the changes, especially so that these do not distort the setter's original intentions. Now, at last, the final draft can be agreed and sent to the Authority for printing.

Even after this, occasionally a few details are altered while checking proofs, as seeing the papers again after some months changes our perspective. The final print is also read by an independent scrutineer, who is asked to read the paper from the candidate's point of view to make certain that all parts of the paper are accurate and make sense. Only after all these processes can the papers be sent to the centres.

You may not like the paper facing your students. You may even feel that for some reason it is unfair. However, you can be sure it has been prepared with great care and with the motive of setting a fair test.

After the Examination – Setting the Standard

When your students stagger out of the examination room, bloodshot of eye and painful of hand, the next stage of the examiners' work is about to begin.

For marking, the scripts are divided into batches of up to ten, which are distributed to a team of markers all over Scotland, each of whom has three weeks to mark an allocation of about 150 Extended Essays or 250 scripts in Paper I or Paper II. Accompanying the scripts are marking instructions, but markers are not left with only written guidance. Before marking their allocations, they attend markers' meetings designed to help them to mark as accurately as possible.

To prepare for the markers' meetings, the examining team reads a random sample of scripts from a range of presenting centres, looking for examples of scripts at different levels of performance. When these have been selected, they are used as the basis for discussion at the meetings. The examiners attempt to reach agreement with the markers on the value of each script, one example representing the standard for a C pass, another for a B, a third for an A, while yet another does not reach the criteria for a pass award. The examining team has used these meetings to encourage markers to overcome the reputation of historians for being unwilling to give very high marks (even full marks!). Remembering that most candidates are 16 or 17 years old, markers are asked to consider what is the best that can reasonably be expected of someone of that age and maturity. That is the standard for the Higher.

Once these standards have been agreed, markers are expected to apply them consistently in marking their own allocations. They are, however, human, so it is necessary to check that this consistency is actually achieved, which is done by the examining team remarking a sample from each marker selected from scripts returned at different stages in the marking process. In carrying out this exercise, the examiners are not worried if a marker is slightly generous or severe, as long as this feature is consistent across the whole batch. In these cases, the marker is given a factor of plus or minus one or more marks, the factor then being applied to all the scripts marked by that marker. The performance of most markers can be standardised fairly easily by this process. In a tiny minority of cases the examiners discover discrepancies in marking which cannot be reconciled in this way. Where this happens, the whole of the marker's allocation is remarked by the examining team. Given the pace at which marking has to be done to meet the deadline for return of scripts, and that it is carried out as an additional task in evenings and at weekends, the accuracy of marking overall is very impressive.

Once the scripts have been marked and the marks have been standardised in this way, it is necessary to consider the overall results of the examination. Only now is it possible to reach a conclusion about the national standard of performance and the difficulty of the examination by comparison with previous years. Three sets of evidence help in reaching this decision: the statistics generated from computer analysis of the standardised marks, the impressions gained by the examiners in reading many hundreds of scripts during the various processes and, at least as significant, the reports made by markers. Markers are asked to include in these reports observations about the overall standard of the scripts in their allocations, to indicate any areas of strength or weakness and any questions which they feel posed particular problems for candidates. These reflections are very helpful in confirming or challenging the indications from the statistics.

All of these factors influence the discussion with the Chief Examiner of the Scottish Qualifications Authority in the meeting at which the pass mark is set to reflect the examiners' conclusions on the quality of performance and the difficulty of the examination. Recalling the observations above on the likely public and political reaction to movements in the pass marks, it must be emphasised that this decision is taken with the greatest of care to fulfil, as nearly as human beings can do so, the criterion that the award of a particular grade in Higher History means the same every year.[2] Remember the sound waves passing overhead . . . ?

Now that the pass mark has been agreed, the final stage can take place, when evidence from centres on behalf of candidates who have been absent from the examination for some reason, or for whom adverse circumstances have been reported, is considered. Only after decisions have been reached on the most appropriate awards in these cases can the marks be processed and certificates printed.

They Think It's All Over . . .

In most countries that would be the end of the matter. In Scotland, however, there is an almost unique system of appeals for candidates whose results did not come up to expectations.

Presenting centres provide the examiners with evidence to support their estimates of performance, in the hope that the examiners will feel that it justifies a higher award. The most important thing about this evidence is that it must support the belief, not that the candidate was capable of achieving a certain standard, but that (s)he had *done so already*. For evidence to be the basis of a successful appeal, it must again fulfil certain criteria in fairness to candidates who have accepted the results awarded to them.

First, it must be equivalent in demand to that required in the national examination. This means that it must contain activities of similar format and level of difficulty, showing that the student has demonstrated the necessary skills at the standard demanded by the national examination and has sustained these over a similar length of test. It follows, therefore, that much shorter assessments, for example those worth only 25 marks instead of 45 in the source based paper, *cannot* be regarded as equally valid to those of full length.

Second, it must be carried out under supervised conditions. Plainly, it would be unfair to candidates whose awards are the result of performance in a timed, invigilated, unseen examination to grant other candidates equal awards on the basis of work carried out at home over an extended period of time and with access to notes, textbooks and other support. That is not equivalence in demand. Although the Scottish Qualifications Authority cannot demand that centres conduct full preliminary examinations, these must be the most convincing sources of evidence for examiners considering appeals.

The process of considering appeals is a lengthy one. Examiners seek to find evidence that the candidate can be considered to have demonstrated the qualities required for the relevant award in two main ways. First, they read the evidence from the centre (sometimes very substantial in quantity!), to assess whether it is strong enough to show that the candidate has, indeed, met the criteria for an enhanced award in work done prior to the examination. If this is not the case, for whatever reason, the examiners then check the marking of the original script to make certain that there have been no errors there. Only after these two processes have been completed may an examiner decide against allowing the appeal.

In cases where centres are disappointed with the outcomes of appeals, these are usually the consequence of either or both of two factors: the nature of the evidence presented and the level of expectation of the centre being unrealistic. Frequently, the material presented does not meet the criteria outlined above, therefore it cannot be used as the basis for an upgraded award. Even where the evidence is in a suitable format, in some centres the marking of internal evidence diverges seriously from national standards, with high marks being awarded for very ordinary work. It is understandable, and quite proper, that teachers seek to encourage candidates, especially in the early months of the course, by giving them marks that they know are higher than the work would receive in an external examination. But it is unrealistic to use these marks as the basis for granting an appeal. Yet this is what appears to be expected in some cases. Alternatively, in some centres the staff do not have an accurate understanding of the standard expected at national level. The resultant disappointment is inevitable.

Throughout the appeals process, as with the procedures following marking, the examining team's first priority is fairness: fairness to those appealing, fairness to those who did not appeal.

. . . It Is Now!

Since the Revised syllabus was introduced in the 1991 examination it has proved, in general terms, to be successful. Teachers appear confident that they know what is expected, even if now and again they dislike particular questions or sources.

This confidence has shown signs of leading to higher standards of attainment, at least in some elements of the examination. The Extended Essay has been the most conspicuous success. Every year markers' reports express satisfaction at the standards they find in these essays, which is as it should be, since it was devised to allow candidates to show off their best work. It has been especially rewarding to find some young historians whose work in these essays is a real pleasure to read and worthy of the highest praise.

As mentioned above, this quality of performance has been less evident in the essays in Paper I, perhaps surprisingly as essay writing has been a feature of History examinations for many years. On the other hand, it has featured much less than formerly in work for other subjects, so perhaps it is natural that students find it difficult to sustain the skills of extended writing under examination conditions. Certainly, the perennial problem remains, which was evident under previous syllabi, that many candidates are content to tell the story in their essays instead of seeking to analyse the historical issue, evaluate the evidence and sustain an argument to reach a relevant conclusion.

Paper II, involving the use of sources, was probably the area which worried teachers most when the new syllabus was introduced. In the first year or two of the examination this was perhaps justified, but in recent years the ability of students to handle sources has improved visibly as people have become more familiar with the demands of the examination. Certain skills are now demonstrated at least fairly well by the majority of candidates: extracting relevant evidence from the sources presented, comparing the views of different authors, evaluating sources on the basis of their provenance and identifying possible bias. In some cases the students also show good grasp of recalled knowledge which they use effectively to evaluate historical events or developments. The greatest potential for further improvement lies in the most difficult of the skills, that of marrying the evidence from the source with that from recalled knowledge to evaluate the viewpoint of the source. Many candidates provide one or both forms of evidence in their answers, but do not make the connections between them. Where this is achieved, the answers reach a new dimension altogether, with able candidates scoring very high marks indeed.[3]

The advent of Higher Still will present new challenges to the examining team. The change in examination format, though based closely on present practice, the novelty of moderating centre marking of internal units, the possibility that there may be a second diet of examinations in December, will all ensure that examiners will continue to experience the old Chinese curse, 'May you have an interesting life'. The guiding purpose will remain, though – to support a system which encourages young people of all ages to study History and which rewards achievement in that study.

On, then, to the future with History. See you there!

Notes

1. Revised Arrangements for Higher History, Scottish Examination Board, (1990), p.8.

2. The Annual Reports of the Scottish Qualifications Authority give the percentage of candidates awarded each grade in the external examinations for every subject.

3. Further details of candidate performance in the external examination can be found in the Annual Reports of the Principal Assessor issued by the Scottish Qualifications Authority.

5

Furth of Scotland –
The European Dimension

Ian McKellar

The complexity and enormity of the European Dimension dictates that this chapter focuses on key recent developments in History teaching in the schools of Europe but it may encourage reflection on the approaches to History teaching in Scotland in a wider context. (For the purposes of this chapter the European context is as defined by the 44 states which take part in the education programmes of the Council of Europe.)[1]

Maitland Stobart defined the Council of Europe's view of History as 'a unique discipline, concerned with a special kind of training of the mind and imagination and with the imparting of an accurate body of knowledge which ensures that pupils understand other points of view'.[2] Such a statement while typical of the Council, is often expressed by its experts in response to ministries of education and curriculum planners to defend History's place in the school curriculum and is usually coupled with the recommendation that all pupils should study History at every level of their education. Indeed in most countries of Europe History is a compulsory subject to age 17–18. Only a few such as the Netherlands and the UK allow it to become a curriculum option after 14, but contemplating the reasons for these variations would lead into interminable discussions of all sorts of factors including the differences in European school systems and their various curricular provisions as well as the value placed on History education itself.[3] Unfortunately there is no room here to explore this fascinating area. But it is a significant question when one tries to assess the place of History in Scottish schools.

Certain characteristics seem to dominate the models for curriculum thinking in school History teaching in Europe and they go some way to explaining how aims and objectives for History are arrived at and defined in different national approaches. These main characteristics can be broadly identified as 'historical consciousness', 'collective memory', and 'national identity – formation', but each tends to become complicated by the knowledge as opposed to skills imperatives that also influence greatly how the subject is taught and learned in Europe.

'Historical consciousness' is generally identified with the Nordic countries (Denmark, Sweden, Norway, and Finland) and Germany. Its appeal lies in its drive to see the past from the standpoint of the present and to help pupils to engage in predicting the future: 'dangerous', maybe, but it certainly adds considerable vitality to the subject at school and provokes and encourages much discussion and debate in senior classrooms: often the oral–discursive powers of pupils become well developed through the resulting pedagogy which encourages a great deal of teacher/pupil and pupil/pupil interaction. One of the contemporary proponents of this approach, Henrik Skovgaard Nielsen, defined historical consciousness as 'an insight into the inter-relationship between interpretations of the past, understanding the present and expectations of the future' and went on to claim that 'History is not the past but the past interpreted by the present and the future'.[4]

Conceptually the approach is very attractive and much of the success and enthusiasm found in Danish History teaching can be attributed to its principles and practice. It has a capacity to excite pupil interest and effectively taught develops intriguingly open–ended historical discussions. Sweden takes this approach also into its upper Secondary Schools as does Finland which defines 'the objective of the study of History is that students see the present as the result of historical development and as the starting point for the future so that they have the possibility to relate their own time and themselves to continuous change and add to their sense of time'.[5] This makes clear how important concepts are. In Sweden too this approach to History influences how museums are set up and how they present their artefacts for interpretation: anyone who has marvelled at the Vasa Museum in Stockholm can attest to the brilliance of its impact. The approach allows even works of fiction to have a place in teaching History. It could be claimed that it was in Germany after 1945 that the concept of historical consciousness was largely developed and emerged in the idea that students and their societies are part of historical processes and that they can influence these processes. However today German History didactics makes a distinction between the unorganised processes of learning (History outside school) and the organised processes (History within school): as far as German History teaching is concerned, the school is the only place where students can study History in a planned and organised way. While the syllabus plans of the 15 Lander show a clear coherence and direction in selection of content, they also vary somewhat in the emphases they take. The exemplar from the Saarland, shown in Table 5.1, is a useful illustration.

As an approach it tends to be more structured than in the Nordics. Nonetheless, the historical consciousness approach might encourage Scottish teachers to revisit how they teach particularly the recent past and compensate for the knowledge deficits in Scottish syllabuses. But of course in many European countries teachers of History are also teachers of Civics or Politics and in some the content taught sometimes integrates.

Type of School	Hauptschule	Realschule	Gymnasium	Gesamtschule
Subject	History	History	History	Social Sciences
Class Level	5 6 7 8 9	5 6 7 8 9 10	5 6 7 8 9 10	5 6 7 8 9 10
No. of Hours	– – 2 2 2	– – 2 2 2 2	– – 2 2 2 2	2 2 2 2 2 2
Content Overview				**Class 5** 1. School Project. 2. Origins of the Earth and Life. 3. Man and Nature. 4. Conqueror & Discoverer.
				Class 6 1. Early Civilisation: Egypt. 2. Freetime – Tourism 3. Water is Life 4. Romans & Celts.
	Class 7 1. Age of Discoveries & Conquests; Reformation and Religious Struggles. 2. Absolutism. 3. European Great Powers 4. American & French Revolutions. 5. Napoleon & Europe 1799–1815.	**Class 7** 1. Prehistoric & Early History. 2. Egypt. 3. Greece. 4. Rome. 5. Middle Ages. 6. France & Islam 7. German Kings & Roman Emperors 8. Medieval society 9. Struggle between Emperor & Pope.	**Class 7** 1. What is History about? 2. Ancient & Early History 3. Egypt. 4. Athenian City State 5. Rome 6. Middle Ages	**Class 7** 1. Middle Ages. 2. Reformation & Peasant's Revolt. 3. Saarland. 4. French Revolution. 5. Childhood & Youth.
	Class 8 1. German Culture 1789–1815 2. Restoration 1815–1848. 3. Revolution in Germany 1848–49. 4. Industrial Revolution. 5. Prussia & Founding of the Reich 1871. 6. Europe in time of Bismarck 7. Imperialism 8. First World War.	**Class 8** 1. Twelfth–century Swabian Kingdom 2. Crusades. 3. The Medieval City. 4. German Eastern Settlement 5. Beginning of Modern Times 6. Reformation & Peasant Revolts 7. Counter – Reformation & Religious Wars. 8. Absolutism. 9. Enlightenment 10. England & North America in the 17th & 18th centuries.	**Class 8** 1. Life in the Middle Ages. 2. Discoveries & Conquests 3. Reformation 4. Absolutism. 5. French Revolution.	**Class 8** 1. Germany 1815–1871 2. Industrial Revolution 3. 'Spaceship Earth' 4. Imperialism & World Issues.
	Class 9 1. Russian Revolution, Communism in the USSR. 2. Weimar Republic. 3. Nazi Dictatorship. 4. Second World War 5. Germany after 1845. 6. European Unity.	**Class 9** 1. Development of Germany in the 19th century. 2. Industrial Revolution 3. First German Reich 1871 4. Imperialism & First World War. 5. Russian Revolution and USSR.	**Class 9** 1. Germany in the nineteenth century. 2. Industrialisation & social change. 3. The Great Powers & World politics.	**Class 9** 1. National Socialism & the Second World War. 2. People and economic awareness. 3. Citizens & State. 4. Germany in Europe.
	Class 10 –	**Class 10** 1. Weimar Republic. 2. National Socialist Dictatorship & Second World War. 3. Germany post 1945. 4. European Integration.	**Class 10** 1. Weimar Republic. 2. National Socialist Dictatorships & Second World War. 3. Germany post 1945 4. Western European integration.	**Class 10** 1. Law & Justice. 2. Peace Education 3. Planning living space.
Additional Material	Regional History and Geographical themes. Family history, Peace and Environmental Themes.	Regional History and Geographical themes. Family history, Peace and Environmental Themes.	Environment, Peace, Women, Family History and I.C.T.	Local and regional history, environment and peace history.

Table 5.1: History Syllabus, Saarland.

'Collective memory' is a peculiarly all-embracing characteristic of many European History syllabuses yet it is usually considered mainly in the context of History-teaching in France where it is quite fundamental and gives the basis for the knowledge parameters of school History. Certainly, specific events have become regarded as indispensable in France as knowledge to be imparted to school pupils: this knowledge ranges across the centuries but would include for instance the Punic Wars, the Battle of Salamis, Alexander the Great's conquests, the French Revolution, the Napoleonic Age, 1848, the Franco-Prussian War, the two World Wars and the more recent wars in Indo-China and Algeria as well as constitutional events like the formation of the IV and V Republics: it suggests a positive attitude to learning about traditional historically significant and national events and to the idea that children should know something of what their parents and grandparents have lived through, and were taught at school themselves. It gives a certainty to the knowledge teachers are expected to cope with, but inevitably it has a traditionally 'national', certainly 'French' ring to it. It is firmly based in 'the importance of the relationship between History teaching and collective identity'. French teachers are loathe to move away from its conceptual framework and in recent times have often battled against ministry proposals intent on introducing more thematic approaches to what is taught. Fundamentally French History teachers see their main purpose in History teaching as a means to *forger une mémoire collective ancrée dans les espaces et les histoires nationales.*'[6]

Jean Peyrot, quite recently retired as President of the 11,000 strong association of teachers of History, Geography and Civics explained *mémoire collective* in the following way:

> Every durable human group is rooted in a past of varying length, but which is always common, made of received and considered memories, some of which have been forgotten, and others turned into landmarks for the present and the future. Human groups in general and political groups in particular, have their special memories which they make their own. Thus there exist memories of families, of villages, or religious groups, of social groups (artisans, peasants etc.) of regions, of nations . . . But these memories are not History as we understand today. History rather is these conflicting memories; the exploration and inventory of these inheritances.[7]

Unquestionably this gives us a clear statement of the philosophical basis of 'collective memory' and provides History teachers in France with the flag round which they have rallied for years! Even critics of such traditionalism like Audigier have had to admit the power of this single characteristic in formulating French History syllabuses:

> in France History is an essential discipline for providing the younger generation with a collective identity and through that to transmit to it a sense of belonging:

a past which shows progressive construction of the nation and territory, with a break at the moment of the French Revolution which signifies a new era marked by progress and political participation. This has two major consequences: syllabuses must be national since they must transmit a shared culture and chronological continuity imposes itself as the main organising principle of these syllabuses since they must show how the present is the consequence of a long evolution.[8]

And only once this is effectively taught will French History teachers contemplate widening the syllabus to European or World parameters! It remains the driving force for what is taught in French schools. To some extent the same important characteristic is found rooted in German and Italian History syllabuses.

A third significant characteristic and currently extremely important particularly in central and eastern Europe is associated with 'national identity formation'. The impulse for this is obviously related to or determined by political circumstances and there have been in the past some quite unpalatable interpretations and results from it. But in very recent times national identity has re-entered the frame for determining the selection of content knowledge in History syllabuses. Knowledge of significant national events is seen as fundamental to the child's upbringing, in turn encourages a sense of belonging and is regarded as valuable for defending and developing cultural awareness. Most European History syllabuses tend to reflect these attributes but syllabuses vary in the proportion devoted to 'national' History. Even in the reputedly liberal, multicultural Netherlands, for instance, it figures largely: some 50 per cent of the final national exam concerns itself solely with Dutch or 'national' History. Most western states make national History their steer too but most also tend to try to teach the national events within a European and sometimes World context. But the more one moves eastwards the more there seems to be concentration on teaching national History; indeed in some of the states formerly within the USSR there is a definite trend towards national History as a 'must' for all pupils. More importantly, perhaps, is that this characteristic has helped to push History into the curricular limelight in these states. This was the message the President of Hungary, Arpad Gonez presented when he opened the European Standing Conference of History Teachers' Assembly (EUROCLIO) and Conference in Budapest in 1997. While it is wonderfully reassuring that History is alive and well and has won this place in the syllabuses of the 'new' European states, there is concern at what exactly is being taught as 'national-identity' making. For instance, Ruman and Vitez recognise this when commenting on Slovakian History-teaching:

national History and the question of Slovak statehood is a central concern, and with it the cultural heritage of a millennium marked by Hungarian rule, the Habsburgs, the Austro-Hungarian Monarchy and by the Czechoslovak Republics before and after World War II . . . the difficulty of limiting the subject by imposing a narrowly conceived Slovak perspective has been very obvious . . .' [9]

and they conclude:

. . . the break-up of History that followed the break-up of the Czechoslovak Federation has been accompanied by attempts to reconstruct national History. So far, however, the search has not led to anything approaching a sufficiently open and comprehensive historical view. We have yet to come upon a solution that strikes the right balance between the emphasis on national uniqueness and pride on the one hand, and historical embeddedness on the other . . . [10]

For several years and in particular in the mid-1990s the Council of Europe and other like-minded agencies such as EUROCLIO, the Koerber Foundation of Hamburg, the Georg Eckert Institute for International Textbook Research at Braunschweig and Kultur Kontakt in Vienna have been engaged in providing seminars and workshop programmes for central and eastern Europe which attempt to encourage 'balanced' approaches to the role and content of History teaching, to produce a 'History without Hatred' in the reform of History teaching in schools, and address the confidence-building of teachers freed from Marxist-Leninist constraints. However, it is among these 'new' states, resulting from the collapse of the Soviet Union, that the impulse towards 'national identity' tends to be strongest, and while there is probably some legitimate room for a revival of national identity in History, examination of the syllabuses so far produced, seems to suggest that 60–80 per cent of all History teaching is to be taken up by national History. Ecker is right to warn that:

we may be allowed to tremble at the spectre of crude nationalisms prevalent in politics and invading History classes. [11]

Behind the national identity-formation approaches there lies the imperative of course to rid the History syllabuses of the former Soviet states of their Marxist-Leninist, even Stalinist, constraints. An early draft of the Standards of History for Georgia for instance proclaimed:

violence of the Soviet totalitarian regime upon the science of History, dogmatic discussion and often distortion of historical facts, ruin of normal education of History in school, and the hardest situation existing in transitive period, at the same time obligation of answering various actual questions – form a lot of difficulties in teaching History in comprehensive secondary school. [12]

This finds an echo in a perhaps more refined way in Rohmer-Stanner's reference to what teachers in Brandenburg (formerly in GDR) had to pursue as late as 1985:

the task of History education is to contribute significantly to the formation of a Marxist-Leninist view of History and a socialist historical consciousness of the pupils, to provide the basis of their class consciousness through a historical viewpoint as well as to help them gain firm Marxist-Leninst attitudes towards the problems of our time and to promote a readiness of the pupils to strengthen and protect the G.D.R. as their socialist fatherland, a readiness which is rooted in the best traditions of German History.[13]

Such a policy allowed the last Minister of Education for GDR, Margot Honecker, to claim:

From Rostock (in the North) to Zwickau (in the South) all children learn the same things in the same way on the same day.[14]

While the new History syllabuses intend to eradicate these stultifying mechanistic Stalinist approaches, it has fallen to the Council of Europe and the other bodies already mentioned to temper enthusiasms for developing 'national' oriented syllabuses. Thankfully it seems more 'balanced' syllabuses are being drawn up: for instance in Slovenia the History syllabus works from the assumption that the main interest in History is to show the transformations of human society in its many eras and varieties and students are expected to be more acquainted with main trends, institutions, events, situations and images, and should recognise existing problems in their many forms, durations and varieties throughout History. Among Georgians, Azerbaijanis and Armenians there are signs of collaborative efforts to produce syllabus guidelines that respect all their various points of view about History and may even allow a Transcaucasian or common History to be taught without nationalistic rancour . . . New curricula frameworks in Poland favour problem-centred and comparative approaches as well as regional and cultural History.[15] Even amidst the equally controversial and tragic histories of Estonia, Latvia, Lithuania and the Ukraine, multi-perspectives are being introduced to temper the nationalistic fervour of the initial attempts at syllabus reconstruction in the early 1990s. In Russia, itself, while new standards are in preparation and yet to appear amid the complexities of developing education systems, more and more teachers are convinced that Russian pupils need to be made more aware of world History, that the old navel-gazing must end and while 'national dignity' is an important concern in their work they have to avoid teaching a 'narrow nationalism'.[16]

Perhaps one of the most succinct statements of a balanced view of the national identity aspect of History is to be discovered in the National Core Curriculum of Hungary (published in 1996):

History, as knowledge of the past, is one of the most important bases of national and European identity, being the collective memory of a society. It is also the lesson of History that peoples and nations are mutually dependent on each other and this mutual dependence requires a global perspective, the discovery of and respect for the diversity and particular heritage of different cultures.[17]

A brief glance at this exemplar page from the documentation for Class 10 shows clearly how the elements of national, European and world History are 'balanced' alongside environmental education, physical and mental education and communication culture:

ATTAINMENT TARGETS

KNOWLEDGE	SKILLS	MINIMUM COMPETENCY
Hungary from the Great Depression to the collapse in the Second World War Years of the Great Depression, end of consolidation. Revisionist foreign policy supported by Nazi Germany. The regime swings to the right. Hungary in the Second World War. German occupation of Hungary. Holocaust, genocide, The Arrowcross terror. Further names, concepts and dates to remember: Gyula Gömbös, Count Pál Teleki, Vienna Awards, 1941, forced labour service, anti-Jewish legislation, Voroniezh, shuttlecock policy, 19th March 1944, ghetto, deportation, 15th October 1944, Ferenc Szálasi.	*Describe the consequences of the Great Depression on the evidence of literary extracts and contemporary sociology works.* **2.IB** *Discuss why the majority of Hungarian society thought revisionism just and rightful, and how it led Hungary into the trap of following German policy.* **3.ID** *Describe the reasons and consequences of the German occupation of Hungary.* **2.IIIA**	Show the results of the territorial revision on a map. War destruction and casualties in Hungary.
The Latest Age A divided World. Power blocks, wars and cold war. Disarmament and thawing. Dissolution of the colonial system. Conditions of the "developing" countries and the North-South question. World economy. Development of the United States and Western Europe. European integration. Communist regimes. Fall of the Communist regimes. Conflicts in the Middle-East. The Far-East (Japan, China). Science, technology, education and culture, way of life at the end of the 20th century.	*Compare the after-war situation of Central Europe with its pre-war conditions.* **5.IA** *On the basis of statistics make a summary of the most important factors of the internationally prevailing power of the USA.* **3.IC** *Explain the concept of Cold War.* **3.IB** *Collect information on how the one-time colonies developed after their achieving independence.* **2.IA** *Make a summary of the work of some organisations in European integration.* **3.IIIB** *Examine the changes initiated by the XX Congress of the Russian Communist Party.* **2.IIB** *Make a comparative chronological chart on the main events of international politics in the 1953-1990 period.* **4.IIIB** *Give own opinion on what caused the fall of the communist regimes.* **2.IIIA** *On the evidence of documents, demonstrate China's significance in international politics.* **2.IIIB**	The UN. Features of the Cold War. Liberation of colonies. The European Union. Fall of the communist regimes.

The signs indicate cross curricular objectives in school education as follows:

⊕	Homeland
⊛	Integration into Europe
⊕	Integration into the World
✳	Environmental Education
⮂	Communication Culture
✕	Physical and Mental Education
▭	Learning
⍲	Career Orientation

In the new states of central and eastern Europe as in western ones, much depends on the textbooks and on the pedagogical approaches they contain and also on methods advocated in the national teaching guidelines. Although Low-Beer has rightly pinpointed many of the current issues about textbooks in her article on 'Creating school History textbooks after Communism'[18] the form of national History is merely one concern among many as she covers the technical state of publishing, market forces, and the economic price of texts as well as the influence – sometimes extending to control – Ministries of Education have over school texts especially in History. But since she wrote in 1997 all over central and eastern Europe there are promising signs today of energetic development of new textbooks many accompanied or supplemented by pupil workbooks. Some containing maps and source extracts pertinent to the analysis of historical events have appeared in countries such as the Czech and Slovak Republics, Estonia, Latvia, Hungary and recently too in Russia. In some western states too, such as Spain, there have been moves to include sources and open up textbooks to more lively and generally more advanced ways of developing thinking in the construction of activities. Sometimes the textbooks include coloured illustrations and while some remain quite encyclopaedic in character they are finding a welcome in hundreds of History classrooms. Interesting perhaps for Scots, is that the most significant aspect of these new textbooks is their inclusion of sources and the desire to pursue open-ended more critical thinking approaches in the accompanying pedagogy. The sample pages, shown on pages 68 and 69, from recently published Spanish[19] and Russian[20] textbooks show how sources and activities have been integrated into the narrative.

Realistically and perhaps later the knowledge parameters set out in many of the national guidelines or standards for History will be forced to reduce or adjust to allow for more effective teaching of source-handling skills and make room for problem-solving and discussion techniques in the classroom: all in all, History teachers are presented with an exciting challenge and to a

A principios de siglo, el ejército alemán había diseñado un plan de ataque que se presentaba como preventivo para el caso de una amenaza seria. Era el llamado Plan *Schilieffen* y los alemanes estaban convencidos de que, si se aplicaba, la victoria sería rápida y segura.

16 **Observa** el siguiente esquema e intenta describir en qué consistía el Plan *Schilieffen*.

doc 18

El éxito del Plan *Schilieffen* se basaba en el hecho de que Bélgica –país neutral– se rendiría en seguida ante la invasión alemana. Pero al contrario de lo que los alemanes habían previsto, Bélgica resistió heroicamente.

17 ¿Puedes descifrar el mensaje de este chiste publicado en la revista *Punch* el 12 de agosto de 1914?

doc 19

Fuente: *The Modern World 1914-1980*. Ed. Stanley Thornes, pág. 7.

Рисунок, сделанный пражанами на постаменте памятника советским солдатам-освободителям

3. В этой ситуации Госден решил отложить планировавшиеся на сегодня переговоры о валютном золоте.

/Из заявления госсекретаря США Раска
советскому послу А. Н. Добрынину[1]/

Сотрудники Госдена в неофициальных разговорах дают понять, что США признают интересы СССР в Восточной Европе и не допустят, чтобы ЧССР стала причиной конфронтации между великими державами.

/Из сообщения чехословацкого посольства в Вашингтоне[2]/

ФРГ должна предпринять дальнейшие шаги к нормализации отношений со странами социалистического лагеря, что касается границ и Мюнхена.

/Из разговора премьер-министра Франции
М. Кув де Мюрвиля с послом ЧССР[3]/

Такой увидел Прагу в августе 1968 г. немецкий корреспондент

??? Вопросы

1. Какой была реакция стран Запада на введение войск стран Варшавского Договора в прессе?

2. Как вы думаете, на чьей стороне было общественное мнение западных государств?

3. Отличалась ли позиция руководства западных стран от мнений, высказанных в прессе? Если «да», то как вы это можете объяснить и оценить?

??? ЗАДАНИЕ (общее к внешней политике СССР и Запада)

1. Знакомясь с фактами, изложенными в разделе, посвященном внешней политике стран Запада и Востока, постарайтесь понять логику и аргументы каждой из противоборствующих сторон. На вопрос: «Кто виноват?» — каждая сторона называла виновником противоположную. Почему?

2. Читая раздел, подумайте также над мнением бельгийского историка Ивана Ванден Берге: «Я всегда полагал, что благодаря политике «холодной войны»... существовала парадоксальная ситуация: обе стороны — и страны, объединенные под эгидой НАТО, и страны Варшавского Договора — не собирались нападать друг на друга... Но вместе с тем и НАТО, и Варшавский Договор пугали свои страны тем, что противоположная сторона спит и видит, как бы на них напасть. На взаимном страхе росли гигантские административные аппараты, новые технологии, которые никому не были нужны... перед угрозой нападения люди становились более послушными, более управляемыми...»

---

[1] Орлик И. И. Запад и Прага в 1968 г. / По документам архива МИД Чешской Республики // Новая и новейшая история. 1996. № 3. С. 16.

[2] Там же.

[3] Там же.

profession somewhat accustomed to narrative or traditional approaches to pupil learning this is a new direction.[21] In many of those countries indeed, child-centredness in History learning is now being promoted again. Agencies such as the Council of Europe – particularly with its series of publications on History teaching[22] – have played a role. So also have the others mentioned above. The International Book Development Company and the World Bank especially in less advanced countries have also contributed to the generation of new textbooks, but in many states it has been the efforts of publishing houses and specific programmes such as the Dutch government's Social Transition Programme Central and Eastern Europe (MATRA) that have developed and encouraged new authors. Finance remains a problem everywhere for resourcing schools but the commitment of many little groups of teachers is an admirable compensation. Much of their enthusiasm and hence the re-development of History education has been sustained all over central and eastern Europe by the setting up of new History Teachers' Associations. Moreover, while the members of the new associations enjoy their democratic freedoms, they also relish the challenges of the new standards and guidelines. Some such as Asociace učitelu dějepisu (ASUD) in the Czech Republic has built up a considerable membership: the small energetic group, the Regional Association of Teachers in History and Social Studies (DOBA), in the Western Ukraine has 'twinned' with its Scottish counterpart, the Scottish Association of Teachers of History (SATH); associations in Hungary and Estonia have made a considerable impact too; the Latvians even have their own office in central Riga; an association was set up recently in Moscow . . . all seem capable of leading the development of History teaching in their countries, and they seek to emulate the successes of the older western associations such as the Vereniging Van Docenten in Geschiedenis en Staatsinrichting in Nederland (VGN) in the Netherlands, the Association des Professeurs d'Histoire et Géographie (APHG) in France, the Historical Association (HA) in the United Kingdom and SATH in Scotland. Many teachers have become writers of new textbooks while others merely participate in co-operative efforts to advance the teaching and learning of their subject. The parent body EUROCLIO, founded in 1993, has, under the inspirational and enthusiastic Joke van der Leeuw-Roord of the Netherlands, done a great deal to support these young associations and helped to promote the attendance of teachers from central and eastern Europe at seminars and conferences in a host of western cities including Glasgow in 1994 and 1995 and Edinburgh in 1999. Establishing bonds of friendship and support across Europe has been a means also of strengthening and developing the place of History in the various school curricula, encouraging exchange of ideas and opinions and sharing the benefits of experience, materials and teaching methods.

This chapter on aspects of History teaching in Europe has aimed at encouraging the reader to indulge in further research into what is happening in many of the countries that form the Europe of today. An appropriate summing-up could well be within the European Union slogan of 'Unity in Diversity': to an extent History education in Europe has now many common features, goals and directions but within the diversity of the educational systems in the 40 or so states there are still very considerable variations in practices, principles and pedagogy.

Notes

1. Council of Europe – the 40 member states are as follows:

   Albania, Andorra, Austria, Belgium, Bulgaria, Croatia, Cyprus, Czech Republic, Denmark, Estonia, Finland, France, Germany, Greece, Hungary, Iceland, Ireland, Italy, Latvia, Liechtenstein, Lithuania, Luxembourg, Malta, Moldova, Netherlands, Norway, Poland, Portugal, Romania, Russian Federation, San Marino, Slovakia, Slovenia, Spain, Sweden, Switzerland, the former Yugoslav Republic of Macedonia, Turkey, Ukraine, United Kingdom.

   Armenia, Azerbaijan, Bosnia and Herzogovinia, Georgia have guest status. Belarus' guest status was suspended in 1997. 44 states take part in the Council's education programmes.

2. M. Stobart, 'Tensions Between Political Ideology and History Teaching', *EUROCLIO Bulletin No. 6*, 1996.

3. This chart (see Table 5.2 on page 72) offers a sample survey of features of school History teaching. It was compiled by Dr. Jana Huttova of Slovakia and was published in the EUROCLIO Bulletin No. 3, 1995.

4. H.S. Neilsen, 'Potsdam and Its Consequences: History Didactical Reflections', *EUROCLIO Bulletin No. 4*, 1995.

5. Curriculum Programme for Upper Secondary Schools, Ministry of Education, Finland, 1996.

6. Le Bureau Nationale, 'Rencontre APHG/SGEN – CFDT', *Historiens et Géographes No. 321*, December 1988.

7. J. Peyrot, 'Case Studies: France', *EUROCLIO Bulletin No. 6*, 1996.

8. F. Audigier, 'History Teaching from Different Perspectives', *EUROCLIO Bulletin No. 8*, 1997.

9. L. Ruman, G. Vitez, 'The Break-Up of Czecho-Slovak Federation. Is it the Break-Up of History?' *Beiträge zur Historischen Sozialkunde 2*, 1996.

10. Ibid.

11. A. Ecker, 'The Development of History Teaching in Central and Eastern European Countries', *Beiträge zur Historischen Sozialkunde 2*, 1996.

Table 5.2: A Survey of the History Curricula of Various European Countries. Following the Delphi Conference, Dr Jana Huttova undertook a survey for the National Curriculum Board of Slovakia. She sent out 30 questionnaires to countries represented at Delphi and had 19 responses. This table summarises the responses.

		QUESTIONS			
COUNTRY	HISTORY AS A COMPULSORY SUBJECT (AGE)	CENTRALISED CURRICULUM	TIME ALLOCATED (LESSONS PER WEEK)	HOW HISTORY IS ORGANISED IN THE CURRICULUM	PRESCRIBED HISTORY TEXTBOOK
Albania	10–14	Yes	P1, S2-3	chron.	No. They are currently working on new textbooks.
Austria	11–18	Yes	P2, S2	chron. lin. (2x)	No. Teachers can choose from 5-6 textbooks.
Croatia	12–19	Yes	n.a.	chron. lin.	Yes. Teachers may use other materials.
Denmark	8–19	Yes very flexible	P2, S3-4	P. mainly NH S. mainly European and world, not necessarily chron.	No. Textbooks are not used very often.
England	5–14	Yes	Recommended Ages 5–7 1 Ages 7–14 2	them P: 75% NH S: 75% NH	No. Schools are free to choose their own textbooks.
Estonia	11–18	Yes	P2, S2-3	chron. lin. them. (30% NH 70% OH)	Yes. Not enough money is available.
Finland	11–18	Yes	P2, S2	chron. lin. them.	No. More textbooks are available.
France	7–17	Yes	P?, S2-3	chron. lin. optional themes	Yes. Teachers have a choice.
Greece	10–18	Yes	P2, S2	chron. them. (6th year), lin. (S)	Yes. There is current discussion about optional texts.
Hungary	10–18	Yes	P2-3, S2-4	chron. lin. them. (2x)	No. Writing of new books is in progress.
Italy	6–18	Yes	P?, S2-3	chron. P: NH S: 50% NH 50% OH	
Latvia	11–17	Yes	P2, S2	chron. lin.	Yes. New books are coming.
Malta	10–18	Yes	P, S2	chron. mainly NH, as option more European and world history.	Yes. Different materials are used in last 2 years.
Netherlands	5–14	Yes just general	P2, S2	them. current mend back to chron. P: mainly NH, S: mainly European and world.	No. Teachers produce materials for themselves.
Norway	10–17	Yes	P3, S2-3	chron. them.	No. Teachers use a range of materials.
Portugal	6–15	Yes	P1, S3-4	cycles 1-2: NH cycle 3: Eur., world 15-18 themes	No
Romania	10–18	Yes	P2, S1-2	chron. lin.	Yes. Alternative is forthcoming.
Slovakia	11–17	Yes	P2, S2 (in 3rd year just 1)	chron. lin. (2x)	No. Writing of new books is in progress.
Slovenia	11–18	Yes	P2, S2	chron. lin. P 40% NH 60% OH	Yes

12. T. Nikolaishvili and T. Chikvaidze, eds., *State Educational Standard: World History*, (Tblisi, 1997).

13. H. Rohmer-Stanner, 'Establishing Inservice Training for History Teachers in the New German States: the case of Brandenburg'. *Beitrage zur Historischen Sozialkunde 2* 1996.

14. Ibid.

15. q.v. A. Chrzanowski, 'Polish History Textbooks in Times of Democratic Tradition – Present Conditions and Prospects', *Beitrage zur Historischen Sozialkunde 2*, 1996.

16. See A. Shevyrev, 'Developments in Russia – the MIROS Institute', *EUROCLIO Bulletin No. 7*, 1996.

17. National Core Curriculum, ed. J. Setenyi, Ministry of Culture and Education, (Hungary, 1996).

18. q.v. A. Low-Beer, 'Ecrire les Manuels d'historie apres le communisme', *Historiens et Géographes*, No. 359, 1997.

19. M.D. Bosch: *Historia del Mundo Contemporáneo*, (Barcelona, 1998), p.172.

20. J. Kushnereva and T. Tchernikova, '*Illusion and Disillusion in the Sixties*', (Moscow , 1998), p.132.

21. See M. Angvik and B. von Borries, eds., '*Youth and History – A Comparative European Survey on Historical Consciousness and Political Attitudes among Adolescents*', vols A and B, (Hamburg, 1997).

    and

    J. van der Leeuw-Roord, ed., *The State of History Education in Europe*, (Hamburg, 1998).

22. 'The Role of History in the Formation of National Identity', 1995.

    'Against Bias and Prejudice', 1995.

    'The Reform of History Teaching in Schools in European Countries in Democratic Transition', 1995.

    'History Teaching and European Awareness', 1995.

    'History and the Learning of History in Europe', 1996.

    'History Teaching and the Promotion of Democratic Values and Toleration, 1996.

    'Mutual Understanding and the Teaching of European History: Challenges, Problems and Approaches', 1996.

    'The Reform of History Teaching in Schools in the Russian Federation', 1996.

    'The Preparation and Publication of New Textbooks for Schools in European Countries in Democratic Transition', 1996.

6

Furth of Scotland – History Education in the United States

Martin Feldman

Comparative Perspectives

To a foreign observer, the American system of education seems complex and different in structure, organisation and administration compared with most nations. Therefore, before discussion and analysis of History education in the United States, it is necessary to offer a 'snapshot' of the major features of American education.

Perhaps the single most striking characteristic of American education is the decentralised nature of the system. The Constitution gave control of education to the states. In theory, this means that each state maintains its own schools and this could result in 50 different systems in terms of organisation, curriculum, administration and philosophy. However, in practice, American education does not vary much from state to state. Perhaps this is a result of historical development; perhaps it is due to the mobility of the American people. Whatever the reason, American schools are similar, wherever one goes.

But there are features which make the system different from an outsider's perspective. Education is controlled and regulated by each state. There is usually some form of State Department of Education responsible for the organisation and delivery of education in the state. However, control is further decentralised by allowing local school districts to have administrative and financial powers. To a Scottish observer, this may seem similar to the Scottish Office Education and Industry Department and the local authorities. But the degree of control that the Scottish Office Education and Industry Department represents throughout Scotland has no counterpart in the USA. If we were to consider Scotland as one of the 50 states, then the role of the Scottish Office Education and Industry Department would be similar to a State Department of Education. The significant feature of this decentralised model is that the role of the Federal government in Washington, D.C. is limited.

The Federal government can offer advice, provide information and recommendations, but cannot directly control and legislate for education. Over the years, the US government provided money and land grants which helped create colleges and universities. In the 1960s, when concern over standards was at fever pitch due to the Russian 'sputnik', the Federal government offered grants for refurbishing and expanding laboratories in schools, provided money for texts and funded summer courses for teachers to update skills and knowledge. But this was all they could do. The states could accept the money, but they still maintained control over the day-to-day delivery of education and how the money was used.

The other major characteristic of American education, which is the result of the decentralised nature of the system, is that there is no national curriculum, nor any national system of exams. Each state monitors and evaluates the programmes in its schools, but each school or school district interprets the state curriculum with a great deal of flexibility and the individual school prepares and presents exams for pupils in the school. This makes it extremely difficult to compare results within a state and almost impossible to compare results throughout and across the country. Only New York State provides a series of state-wide exams for Secondary Schools. The significance of this decentralised control of schools affects many aspects of American education.[1]

History in the Curriculum

The curriculum is the responsibility of each state – and references to 'the History curriculum', or 'the English curriculum', for example, must indicate which state is being referred to. There is a wide variety of topics and approaches in the History curriculum across the country, yet in spite of this diversity, there is a basic similarity common to all.

The key factor which must be considered when examining the History curriculum in the US is that at one level there is no such thing as a History curriculum. History is only one part of a wider subject, called Social Studies, which includes History, Geography, Politics, Economics and World Cultures. However, History is perhaps the key player in Social Studies as it represents the major portion of the Social Studies programme. The majority of teachers have studied or 'majored' in History during their undergraduate years.

The Social Studies programme and the teaching of Social Studies adopts a multi-disciplinary approach. Different topics and themes are slotted into different years of the school curriculum. A topic may be subject specific or may adopt a multi-disciplinary approach, depending upon the focus and aims of the topic. There are no separate departments of History, Geography or Modern Studies. There is a department of Social Studies in each Secondary School. There are teachers of Social Studies and the syllabus – from

Kindergarten through to Grade 12 – includes Social Studies as a major component.

Teachers in the United States are required by each state to take a range of subjects to qualify as a teacher of Social Studies. History, both American and World History, is usually a basic requirement. Some Geography, World Cultures (Anthropology and Sociology), Politics and Economics are all required as part of the subject background preparation. Teachers do specialise, but if an American teacher is asked about his or her subject background, he probably would not say he/she is a historian or a geographer, rather a teacher of Social Studies.

Social Studies cannot be compared to any subject in the Scottish curriculum. In some ways it is similar to Modern Studies, but does not adopt the post-1950s emphasis of that subject. Social Studies is perhaps similar to the Social Subjects section of the 5–14 Environmental Studies programme – yet does not have similar aims and objectives.

It would be useful to examine more closely, but still rather briefly, just what is meant by the term 'Social Studies'.

Social Studies

What is Social Studies? In 1992, the Board of Directors of the National Council for the Social Studies, the major organisation for Social Studies educators, adopted the following definition:

> Social Studies is the integrated study of the social sciences and humanities to promote civic competence. Within the school program, Social Studies provides co-ordinated, systematic study drawing upon such disciplines as anthropology, Archaeology, Economics, Geography, History, Law, Philosophy, Political Science, Psychology, Religion and Sociology... The primary purpose... is to help young people develop the ability to make informal and reasoned decisions for the public good as citizens of a culturally diverse, democratic society in an interdependent world.[2]

It is taught in kindergarten through Grade 12 (Secondary Year 6) in schools across the nation. It is multi-disciplinary and inter-disciplinary and sometimes in one class called 'Social Studies' and sometimes is taught in separate discipline-based classes within a department of Social Studies.

Two main characteristics define Social Studies; it is designed to promote civic competence and it is integrative, incorporating many subjects and disciplines. The National Council for the Social Studies(NCSS) emphasises the following:

1. Social Studies have as a major purpose the promotion of civic competence – which is the knowledge, skills and attitudes required of students to be able to assume the role of citizen...

2. K-12 Social Studies integrates knowledge, skills and attitudes within and across disciplines.

3. Social Studies programmes help students construct a knowledge base and attitudes drawn from academic disciplines or specialised ways of viewing reality.[3]

The manner of organising and integrating concepts and processes from different disciplines varies with the level of the school. In elementary school, Social Studies is taught in the form of units constructed around themes – similar to the project work in Scottish Primary Schools. As children move up through school, programmes may continue to be integrated and inter-disciplinary. Alternatively, classes can be linked to specific disciplines, for example, a History course. But always the classes draw upon concepts and material from other social sciences.

In 1992 the NCSS, after long discussion and with much disagreement and criticism, produced a report which outlined 10 themes that would form the framework of the Social Studies standards:

1. Culture.
2. Time, Continuity and Change.
3. People, Places and Environments.
4. Individual Development and Identity.
5. Individuals, Groups and Institutions.
6. Power, Authority and Governance.
7. Production, Distribution and Consumption.
8. Science, Technology and Society.
9. Global Connections.
10. Civic Ideals and Practices.[4]

This report elaborated in some detail on each theme and included a chapter for the early grades (up to Primary 5), middle grades (Primary 6 and Primary 7) and high school (secondary) level. Each theme includes a list of pupil performance expectations (criteria) and classroom activities. This does not appear to be controversial – at least to a Scottish teacher. Yet, there was a tremendous reaction to the report and criticism was strong – and in places, might be described as extremely hostile.

What appeared to be a rather straightforward presentation which had involved discussion and participation from a wide range of members, resulted in numerous letters, articles and papers at conferences. In a sense, this indicates one of the major problems in preparing and developing a curriculum for Social Studies programmes.

There is strong disagreement over different philosophies and objectives of the Social Studies. There are the subject specialists – particularly the historians, who want History to be the foundation of the Social Studies. They argue for the value of History and the importance of History in the school curriculum. Then there are individuals who believe that a study of the social problems of society should be the cornerstone and the key element in the Social Studies. There are others who emphasise critical thinking and take a Deweyan approach to the organisation and goals of the curriculum.[5]

One educator has labelled curriculum as the battleground for competing claims – and this is most certainly the case in any attempt to devise a curriculum for the Social Studies. What exacerbates the problem is the decentralised nature of the American education system. The National Council for the Social Studies is a professional organisation – but it has no legal powers and it merely offers recommendations and suggestions, which are then taken on board as different groups or states see fit.

Consequently, there is a degree of similarity in Social Studies programmes throughout the nation, but there are significant differences in structure, philosophy, organisation and implementation.

Examples of Social Studies Programmes

To help the reader better understand Social Studies curricula in the US, it is useful to offer examples from the programme in three states – New York, Washington and New Jersey. Each is different, yet each contain elements which are similar. They are based upon a 'learning standards' approach and they outline content linked to pupils achieving standards set out in the curriculum.

It is important to remember the excerpts contain only standards and content related to History, since this is the focus of discussion and analysis in this book. The remainder of each programme illustrates the way in which standards in Geography, Economics, World Cultures and Politics will be achieved.

A. STATE OF WASHINGTON

The essential academic learning requirements in History are:

1. The student examines and understands major ideas, eras, themes, developments, turning points, chronology and cause-and-effect relationships in US, world and Washington State History.

To meet this standard, the student will:

1.1 understand historical time, chronology and causation, how events occur in time and place, are sequenced chronologically and impact future events;

1.2 analyse the historical development of events, people, places and patterns of life in US, World and Washington State History;

1.3 examine the influence of culture on US, World and Washington State History.

History Education in the United States

Table 6.1: Social Studies: History – Essential Academic Learning Requirements – State of Washington. The student examines and understands major ideas, eras, themes, developments, turning points, chronology, and cause and effect relationships in US, World and Washington State History.

	COMPONENTS	BENCHMARK 1 – TBD (i)	BENCHMARK 2 – TBD	BENCHMARK 3 – TBD
1.1	Understand historical time, chronology, and causation.	group personal, local and state events by broadly defined historical eras and place in proper sequence on a time line.	group events and individuals by broadly defined historical eras and develop related time lines.	group events and individuals by broadly defined historical eras and use time lines to explain patterns of historical continuity and change in the historical succession of related events.
		use broad categories of time (years, decades, and centuries)	measure time by millennia and calculate calendar time BC and AD.	measure time by millennia and calculate calendar time BC and AD.
		investigate cause and effect relationships of historical events.	rank the importance of causal factors for given events including the possibility of the accidental as a causal factor in history.	work forward from an initiating event to its outcome recognising cause and effect, multiple causation or the accidental as factors in history.
1.2	Analyse the historical development of events, people, places and patterns of life in US., World, and Washington State History.	US HISTORY		
		describe life in the early US both before and after European contact, *for example, land and people before Columbus, exploration and discovery.*	identify and explain major issues, movements, people and events in US history from beginnings to 1877 with particular emphasis on change and continuity, *for example, revolution, the emergence of sectional differences, and the Civil War.*	Identify and analyse major issues, movements, people and events in US History from 1870 to the present with particular emphasis on growth and conflict, *for example, industrialisation, the civil rights movement and the information age.*

Note: the term TBD, after each Benchmark, means 'to be determined'. Generally, a Benchmark is a point in time which may be used to measure pupil progress. Usually, Grade 4 (Primary 5), Grade 7 (Secondary 1) and Grade 10 (Secondary 4).

2. The student applies the methods of social science investigation to investigate, compare and contrast interpretations of historical events.

   To meet the standards the student will:

   2.1 investigate and research
       use sources of information such as *historical documents, eye witness accounts, photos, works of art, letters,* and *artefacts* to investigate and understand historical occurrences;

   2.2 analyse historical information
       evaluate different interpretations of major events in US, World and Washington State History;

   2.3 synthesise information and reflect on findings.

3. The student understands the origin and impact of ideas and technological developments on History and social change.

   To meet this standard, the student will:

3.1 explain the origin and impact of an idea on society for example, *free speech, rule of law*, or *separation of church and state*;

3.2 analyse how historical conditions shape the emergence of ideas and how ideas change over time;

3.3 understand how ideas and technological developments influence people, resources and culture.

B. State of New York

The Resource Guide which accompanies the *Learning Standards for Social Studies* stated that 'it is important to define critical dimensions of teaching and learning that should be to develop curriculum and instruction based on the six standards'.

These dimensions are:
intellectual skills
multi-disciplinary approaches
depth and breadth
unity and diversity
multi-culturalism and multiple perspectives
patterns to organise data
multiple learning environments and resources
student-centred teaching, learning and assessment.

The Resource Guide also outlines key concepts of the K-12 Social Studies program in History, Geography, Economics, Civics and Citizenship. The concepts for History are:

change	involves the basic alterations in things, events and ideas;
choice	means the right or power to select from a range of alternatives;
culture	means the patterns of human behaviour that includes ideas, beliefs, values, artefacts and ways of making a living which any society transmits to succeeding generations to meet fundamental needs;
diversity	means understanding and requesting of others and oneself, including similarities and differences in language, gender, socio-economic class, religion and other human characteristics and traits;
empathy	means the ability to understand others through being able to identify in one's self responses similar to the experiences, behaviours and responses of others;
identity	means awareness of one's own values, attitudes and capabilities as an individual and as a member of different groups;
imperialism	means the domination by one country of the political and/or economic life of another country or region;

movement of people and goods
> refers to the constant exchange of people, ideas, products, technologies and institutions from one region or civilisation to another that has existed throughout History;

Nationalism means the feeling of pride and devotion to one's country of the desire of a people to control their own government, free from foreign interference or rule;

Urbanisation means movement of people from rural to urban areas.

The curriculum sets out Leaving Standards for Social Studies at three levels – elementary (Primary 1-5), intermediate (Primary 6 – Secondary 1), and commencement (Secondary School from Secondary 2 – Secondary 6). Standards 1 and 2 focus on History, with Standard 1 dealing with United States and New York History and Standard 2 studying World History. Standards 3, 4 and 5 concentrate on Geography, Economics and Civics and Government.

Standard 1: History of the United States and New York.

> Students will use a variety of intellectual skills to demonstrate their understanding of major ideas, eras, themes, developments and turning points in the History of the United States and New York.

Standard 2: World History

> Students will use a variety of intellectual skills to demonstrate their understanding of major ideas, eras, themes, developments and turning points in World History and examine the broad sweep of History from a variety of perspectives.

---

4. The skills of historical analysis include the ability to:

> explain the significance of historical evidence;
>
> weigh the importance, reliability, and validity of evidence;
>
> understand the concept of multiple causation;
>
> understand the importance of changing and competing interpretations of different historical developments.

Students:

- analyse historical narrative about key events in New York State and United States History to identify the facts and evaluate the authors' perspectives;

- consider different historians' analyses of the same event or development in United States History to understand how different viewpoints and/or frames of reference influence historical interpretations;

- evaluate the validity and credibility of historical interpretations of important events or issues in New York State or United States History, revising these interpretations as new information is learned and other interpretations are developed.

Adapted from National Standards for United States History

Table 6.2: Excerpt from Commencement, Standard 1.

THE UNITED STATES EXPANDS ITS TERRITORIES AND BUILDS AN OVERSEAS EMPIRE

OBJECTIVES:

1. to understand how and why the United States grew during the 19ᵗʰ century.
2. to recognise that American territorial and economic growth had widespread economic, political, and social impacts both at home and abroad.
3. to describe the reasons for periodising history in different ways.
4. to understand the relationship between the relative importance of United States domestic and foreign policies over time.
5. to analyse the role played by the United States in international politics, past and present.
6. to compare and contrast different interpretations of key events and issues in New York State and United States History and explain reasons for these different accounts.

CONTENT OUTLINE:

A   Growth of Imperialist Sentiment Was Cause By Several Factors:

1. a belief that the nation had a right to the land, i.e., Manifest Destiny – 'people's differing perceptions of places, people and resources';
2. perceived moral obligations to extend America's way of life to others, i.e., ethnocentrism and racism;
3. American citizens were already migrating into new lands in North America – the effects of human migration on the characteristics of different places;
4. increased foreign trade led to a growing interest in gaining control over some foreign markets;
5. fear that other foreign nations would gain control of strategic locations at the expense of the United States;
6. developing technology in transportation and communication contributed to American expansion potential – the importance of location and certain physical features;

B   The Spanish-American War Signalled the Emergence of the United States as a World Power.

1. the war's origins lay in Cuban attempts to gain freedom from Spain;
2. United States' concerns, i.e., pro-expansionist sentiment, Cuba's location, Spanish tactics;
3. newspapers shaped public opinion over the Maine incident – "yellow journalism";
4. conduct of the war created domestic and international problems;
5. opposition to American imperialist movement.

C   Victory in the Spanish-American War created a Need for a New Foreign Policy

1. acquisition of land far from America's shores – importance of resources and markets;
2. emphasis on doing what the government felt was necessary and possible to protect American interests, i.e., maintaining a strong navy, gaining control of other strategic locations, advocating equal trading rights in Asia, e.g. the Open Door Policy;
3. actions created conflict with Filipinos and Japanese.

D   United States Policies in Latin

1. The United States attempted to control a number of locations in Latin America for economic and political reasons;
2. the quest for Latin American stability through the Roosevelt Corollary to the Monroe Doctrine;
3. armed intervention in Latin America.

Table 6.3: Excerpt from a Two Year Sequence of Study, Grades 7–8

C. State of New Jersey

There are nine Social Studies standards which deal separately with History, Geography, Civics and Economics. Teaching to the standards must be based on three considerations:

1. *Focusing on the specific language of the standards and indicators.* Each indicator must be considered as a separate entity, and a way to focus on the subject studied.
2. *More comprehensive coverage and depth of context than in the pre-standards era.* The standards will require greater vigour and specificity in the treatment of topics.
3. *Teaching methods based on the most current theory and research.*

The nine standards are:

6.1 All students will learn democratic citizenship and how to participate in the constitutional system of government of the United States.

6.2 All students will learn democratic citizenship through the humanities, by studying literature and History, Philosophy and related fields.

6.3 All students will acquire historical understanding of political and diplomatic ideas, forces and institutions throughout the history of New Jersey, the United States and the World.

6.4 All students will acquire historical understanding of societal ideas and forces throughout the History of New Jersey, the United States and the World.

6.5 All students will acquire historical understanding of varying cultures throughout the History of New Jersey, the United States and the World.

6.6 All students will acquire historical understanding of the economic forces, ideas and institutions throughout the history of New Jersey, the United States and the World.

6.7 All students will acquire geographical understanding by studying the world in spatial terms.

6.8 All students will acquire geographical understanding by studying human systems in Geography.

6.9 All students will acquire geographical understanding by studying the environment and society.

National Standards for History

In the 1980s, several government reports were published which voiced concern about low standards and poor achievement in American Schools. These reports reflected increasing concern and uncertainty about the Schools and stimulated discussion and government intervention, at national and state

---

THE PHARAOHS OF ANCIENT EGYPT

HISTORICAL PERIOD(S):   PREHISTORY (TO 2000 BC)
HISTORICAL THEME(S):   HISTORY OF RELATIONS BETWEEN POLITICAL GROUPS AND
ENTITIES
HISTORY OF POLITICAL LEADERSHIP

ACTIVITY:

In examining the development of Egyptian civilisation, students should identify the contributions of the pharaohs in areas such as law, taxation, trade and military stability. Students can develop a spreadsheet or database comparing the accomplishments of Egyptian pharaohs. Some examples are Menes, Queen Hatshepsut, Thutmose III, Amenhotep IV (Akenaton), and Ramses II. In lower grades, students can visit a museum of Egyptian artefacts (e.g. The American Museum of Natural History in New York City; also, The Temple of Dendur at the Metropolitan Museum of Art) to observe the wealth and technology of this civilisation. Teachers should explain the importance of a stable political authority in providing the resources for this wealth.

FURTHER EXPLORATION:

Advanced students may explore the rich literature of Ancient Egypt. Through reading *The Inscription of Amenemhet*, or selections from *The Book of the Dead* and *The Tale of Sinuhe*, students can acquire understanding of Egyptian mythology and religion.

CONNECTIONS:

This topic can be connected to diplomatic objectives of Standard 6.3 through the teaching of the Egyptian invasions of the Kush, Sudan, Syria, and Palestine. By using spreadsheets and data bases to organise information on Egyptian civilisation, students can improve their computer skills.

Workplace Readiness Standard 2, Indicators 6, 7, and 8.

Table 4: Excerpt from Standard 6.3, New Jersey

levels. This dissatisfaction resulted in almost every state initiating a wide-ranging reform and revision of curriculum. The new programmes were based upon a learning standards approach, incorporated new interpretations and content and included directions and instruction for assessment.

Social Studies' programmes were included in these revisions and reform. In addition to state initiatives, there was a major attempt to develop a nation-wide consensus which would support a History programme which would be adopted by the states. In Spring 1992, the National History Standards Project was established, and the National Centre for History in the Schools was established at the University of California at Los Angeles. It was funded by the National Endowment for the Humanities and the United States Department of Education. The Centre included teachers, advisors and historians and after wide-ranging consultation, two books were published in autumn 1994 – *National Standards for United States History* and *National Standards for World History*.

These reports were met with an unexpected storm of criticism and the reaction was so strong that the United States Senate voted 99 to 1 to reject them, even though the Federal government had no control over education. The reports were revised and modified and in 1996 a new volume was published, *The National Standards for History, Basic Edition,* which combined the United States History and World History Standards in one volume. It must be remembered that these Standards represent the views and ideas of a private organisation and are not binding on any state and any curriculum.[6]

However, it would be useful to include some comments, themes and sections from this publication as it does represent a position and offers insight into a History curriculum which has support from a significant group in the United States.

STANDARDS IN HISTORICAL THINKING

1. Chronological thinking.
2. Historical Comprehension.
3. Historical Analysis and Interpretation.
4. Historical Research Capabilities.
5. Historical Issues – Analysis and Decision-making.

These Standards indicate a concern and interest in the process of Historical thinking. For United States History and World History, the publication outlines a topical approach, using the term 'Era' as an organising device. World History and United States History have been divided into 10 eras.

WORLD HISTORY

Era 1: The Beginnings of Human Society

Era 2: Early Civilisations and the Emergence of Pastoral Peoples, 4,000–1000 BCE.

Era 3: Classical Traditions, Major Religions and Giant Empires, 1000 BCE–300 CE.

Era 4: Expanding Zones of Exchange and Encounter, 300–1000 CE.

Era 5: Intensified Hemispheric Interactions, 1000–1500 CE.

Era 6: The Emergence of the First Global Age, 1450–1770.

Era 7: An Age of Revolution, 1750–1914.

Era 8: A Half Century of Crisis and Achievement, 1900–1945.

Era 9: The Twentieth Century Since 1945: Promises and Paradoxes.

Era 10: World History Across the Eras.

DETAILED EXAMPLE:

Era 7:   An Age of Revolution, 1750–1914.

Overview

Standard 1: the causes and consequences of political revolution in the late eigteenth and early nineteenth centuries.

Standard 2: the causes and consequences of the agricultural and industrial revolutions, 1700–1850.

Standard 3: the transformation of Eurasian societies in an era of global trade and rising European power, 1750–1870.

Standard 4: patterns of nationalism, state–building, and social reform in Europe and the Americas, 1830–1914.

Standard 5: patterns of global change in the era of Western military and economic domination 1800–1914.

Standard 6: major global trends from 1750–1914.

DETAILED SECTION

Standard 4: patterns of nationalism, state-building and social reform in Europe and the Americas 1830–1914.

4a: the student understands how modern nationalism affected European politics and society.

4b: the student understands the impact of new social movements and ideologies in nineteenth-century Europe.

Therefore, the student is able to:

(Grades 5–12) Analyse causes of large-scale migrations from rural areas to cities and how these movements affected the domestic and working lives of men and women.

(Grades 7–12) Explain the leading ideas of Karl Marx and analyse the impact of Marxist beliefs and programs on politics, industry and labour relations in later nineteenth-century Europe.

(There are 5 additional sections of 4b and these are followed by 4c and 4d, each of which contains additional sections which outline pupil expectations).

Lessons for Scotland?

This chapter has outlined the major features of American education, described the nature and meaning of the Social Studies programmes and presented examples of History curricula in the United States. The analysis demonstrates that despite developing in isolation there have been parallel developments in the United States and Scotland. Furthermore, the teaching of History in the United States provides some pointers for future developments in History teaching in Scotland.

It is apparent that although there is no national curriculum in History, there is a broad consensus which results in similar programmes throughout the nation. This mirrors the popularity of certain topics in Scottish Schools set within a more flexible set of curriculum structures. It is also evident that all new programmes are learning standards based, with content outlined and linked to pupil achievement which is the basis of assessment. This finds parallels in the strands and targets within Environmental Studies 5–14 and the outcomes and performance criteria for Higher Still. Scotland is not alone in having developed an assessment driven method of teaching.

In Chapter 12 of this volume, Jim McGonigle outlines the arguments for and against an integrated approach to the teaching of social subjects. In the United States, despite the existence of Social Studies departments, History remains a clearly identifiable subject with a separate syllabus and assessment criteria. This may give weight to the argument that Scottish Schools should not go down the integrated route for the delivery of social subjects but that each subject, including History, should retain its own identity with the subsequent commitment and loyalty of History teachers.

Both Scotland and the United States balance national history with a world view. However, the United States takes a more chronological and structured approach to the teaching of its History and as both Moira Laing and David Duncan note in this volume, there are strong arguments suggesting that Scotland should rationalise the teaching of its History. Finally, an overt aim of History teaching in the United States is to engender a commitment to democracy and prepare people to play an active role in American society. While many History teachers in Scotland would support these aims, they would see their role more in terms of raising issues and when analysing past political systems giving pupils the opportunity to discuss and debate the respective advantages and disadvantages.

Notes

1. There are no recent books which outline the organisation and administration of American Education. The classic text by Edmund J. King, *Other Schools and Ours*, (New York, 1973, 4th edition is no longer available).

   Richard P. Adams, *Lessons from Abroad*, (Lancaster, Pennsylvania, 1995). Is interesting and contains useful information, but lacks the analysis and detail of the King book.

2. Expectations of Excellence, Curriculum Standards for Social Studies, National Council for the Social Studies, (Washington, D.C., 1994), pp.2–3.

3. Ibid.

4. Ibid.

5. See Martin Feldman, and Eli Seifman, (eds), *The Social Studies: Structure, Models, Strategies*, (New Jersey, 1969), particularly Section 2, which contains articles presenting different philosophies of Social Studies. For a classic text which offers a detailed presentation of reflective thinking and a problem approach as the basis for Social Studies, see Maurice Hunt and Lawrence Metcalf, *Teaching High School Social Studies*, (New York, 1968).

6. A fascinating and valuable book has been written by the co-directors of the National Centre for History in the Schools. Gary Nash, Charlotte Crabtree and Ross E. Dunn, *History on Trial: Culture Wars and the Teaching of the Past*, (New York, 1997). The authors describe the controversy which followed the publication of the first two volumes and offer a detailed and revealing insight into curriculum development.

7

Meeting Pupils' Needs – Issues of Differentiation in the Learning and Teaching of History

Sydney Wood

Introduction

When Amy Stewart Fraser attended an Aberdeenshire school in the 1900s, her History lessons consisted of memorising 'strings of dates of battles and sieges, the reigning years of monarchs and Acts of Parliament'.[1] Popular perception still probably sees History like this. Historians are useful members of pub quiz teams. When strong memories of History lessons remain, then autobiographical evidence suggests this is due to the eccentricities of teachers and their vivid and personalised style of teaching the subject. In 1940s' Aberdeen David Hay attended the Grammar School where just such a teacher operated: 'My memory of her is constituted by her presentation of a series of vignettes of History in which the iniquities of the English were made vividly clear to us. To this day my knowledge of Scottish History is no more than a vague chauvinistic haze permeated by hostility to England and populated by Bruce, Wallace, Knox, the Covenanters, Mary Queen of Scots and Bonnie Prince Charlie'.[2]

These images of a History immediately accessible to all have been severely dented by upheavals since the 1960s. Academic historians have been endlessly troubled by challenges to the objectivity of knowledge and by arguments that historical texts are contrivances that impose invented order upon the past.[3] The work of the Schools Council in the 1970s is still with us, defining the subject's attributes in terms of complex skills and concepts and requiring assessments that use historical knowledge as the vehicle for demonstrating conceptual understanding and historical skills. Add to this the subject's very heavy use of text and requirements that pupils create text, and it is little wonder that History is often seen by pupils as a difficult subject.

This is, of course, nothing to be ashamed of in a world where 'dumbing down' is a phrase often applied to educational standards, and where the Juggernaut of modularisation rolls over all who cry out that lengthy sustained study is desirable. But History classes commonly contain a wide spread of ability. How can all be appropriately challenged and extended without being overwhelmed by what is asked of them? This chapter will survey some of the aspects involved in addressing the issue of differentiation and will describe particular aspects of it explored in research projects in which the author was involved.

Does Differentiation Matter?

In a whole range of writings the journalist Melanie Phillips has raged against the way 'the education system has been subverted by the ideological fixation with false egalitarianism which allows the fear of differentiating between sheep and goats to turn proper pedagogic concerns on their head'.[4] The Scottish Office Education and Industry Department's History inspectors cannot be blamed for holding such a view. In their survey of History teaching in Scotland they assert that teachers must 'take account of the differing starting points at which pupils begin their study of History . . . History teachers should continue to develop strategies which ensure that work is carefully matched to the needs of the pupil'.[5]

There is nothing peculiarly Scottish in this assertion for similar assumptions can be found in official documentation from all parts of the United Kingdom. In 1989 the Scottish Office Education Department indicated that differentiation meant that: 'pupils in a particular class need not study the same things at the same pace and in the same way at all times. Differentiated approaches should mean that the needs of the very able and of children with learning difficulties are discerned and met'.[6]

The official view, then, is that differentiation is a key attribute of good practice. Yet neither the authors of official surveys nor researchers seem convinced that what is currently on offer in the classroom can be regarded as effectively addressing the issue. According to one researcher: 'History teachers need more explicit training in the processes of constructing differentiated tasks and the ways in which such tasks can raise pupil expectations'.[7]

Whether in Primary or Secondary Schools, teachers of History face classes containing wide ranges of ability. Prior to Secondary 3 this tends to be the result of national policies (though there are signs of change here): from Secondary 3 onwards it is the inevitable consequence of the subject's optional status. There is but a minority of schools able to organise History pupils in classes differentiated in terms of ability. Moreover, the curricular documents that guide teachers' work set out History's attributes in differentiated fashion. Scant though practical and constructive guidance might be, differentiation is not an issue that teachers can avoid.

What Aspects of History Need to be Differentiated?

The popular perception of History as a body of memorised knowledge, and the professional perception that it consists of complex skills and a grasp of concepts, itself indicates the scale of the problem. History teachers are faced with differentiating a context in terms of its conceptual demands and devising a context to be the means of developing historical skills. A third strand of the problem is provided by the means used, for History deploys written, visual, aural and mathematical resources each of which pose their own problems. Nor are teachers immune from changing fashions which have in the past pressed upon them such approaches as 'integration', 'resource-based learning', and 'group work' regardless of the confusions and lowering of standards that may result.[8]

It is rare to find work that wrestles with the question of what makes an historical context vary in difficulty. Yet Martin Booth has very properly pointed out the problem of simply seeing History as 'a cognitive skill such as the comprehension or analysis of a written source. The difficulty level will largely be determined by the historical topic'.[9] Just one substantial piece of work offers guidance.[10] Kieran Egan has attempted to relate the attributes of pupils at various stages to the kinds of historical topics best suited to their abilities. He describes pupils up to the age of seven, for example, as being at a 'mythic' stage, lacking experience and knowledge of change and causality on an historical scale, concerned above all with their own mental lives and thus best offered stories that reach clear conclusions and involve simple struggles between opposites (such as rich and poor, courage and cowardice). His analysis accords reasonably well with a major on-going research project that is especially concerned with how children explain the past.[11] The researchers have presented pupils of varying ages with a number of events and circumstances that either offer a puzzle or a practice that is hard to explain in modern terms (such as Roman success in overcoming far bigger numbers of British warriors motivated by defending their homes) and ranked their responses which range from finding the past baffling to appreciating past people in their own terms.

The Attainment Outcome (AO) 'Understanding People in the Past' within the 5–14 programme[12] does attempt to categorise content broadly into three levels of difficulty, but does so without really shedding light on the teaching of a range of ability in one class. Moreover, the second key feature in this AO is inextricably bound up with the one that is most obviously concerned with content, focused, as it is, on the concepts of cause and effect and change and continuity. The assessable element of Standard Grade that deals with the equivalent matters pulls them together as a single statement; yet merely raising the question 'Why did the First World War occur' is evidence enough of the complexities of content knowledge.

Historical skills are concerned, above all, with appreciating the nature of historical evidence and handling historical sources appropriately. The 5–14 programme also raises the matter of understanding historical time and sequence, a relatively well-researched dimension of the subject where investigators have found that careful teaching and content knowledge are crucial and that: 'There is a time language that accompanies the development of the child and it can be described and specifically detailed'.[13]

The ability to extract relevant data from a source is much akin to an English interpretation exercise: it is the issue of source authorship that is critical. The upper levels of the strands of the Social Subjects Attainment Targets, 5–14, indicate that this is necessary by Secondary 1 and 2. Yet such little evidence as we have suggests that this is one of the hardest of ideas for pupils to grasp. An American academic found that 16-year-olds performed poorly when asked to arrange a cluster of sources on the Battle of Lexington in terms of their value to the historian. Whereas historians looked first at the date and authorship of these sources, pupils failed to do this first and failed to appropriately evaluate sources when they did study their provenance. The researcher comments that: 'able high school students can know a lot of History but still have little idea of how historical knowledge is constructed'.[14]

Two more American researchers comment: 'We suggest some caution in the use of primary materials since the research . . . notes that children are not spontaneously critical of narrative sources. Critical analysis needs to be built into instruction'.[15]

The stampede down the source-handling road has raised serious problems. The creators of texts, cartoons, drawings, maps and photographs certainly did not have in mind Scottish adolescents of many years hence as they went about their activities. The intelligibility issue has led some setters of source-based tasks to tweak them into forms their original authors did not intend: this activity, furtive at first, has gradually become quite brazenly common. Nor is this the end of the matter, for we also present pupils with text of modern creation that has been specifically produced for their usage. Is this, too, to be critically evaluated in terms of authorship? It is, perhaps, not surprising that at least one commentator has noticed that pupils read textbooks 'as if their authors did not exist at all, as if they were simply the instruments of a heavenly intelligence transcribing official truths'.[16]

We are very prone to question pupils on the value, accuracy, bias, and reliability of sources. Without contextual knowledge it is impossible to answer such questions other than by listing all the questions one would want answers to before placing any trust in a source's content. Where is such contextual knowledge to come from? When we begin to teach that the very textbooks used to provide it are themselves the creation of flawed and fallible authors with their own purposes, then we are pushing pupils out onto the constantly shifting sea of uncertainty that is historical study. It is little wonder that many of them flounder, some drown, and yet more prefer to avoid putting to sea at all and choose instead the 'scientific certainties' of Geography. 'Traditional' History provided pupils with the coherent flow of secondary text. 'New' History has resulted in fragmented experiences, and in pages spattered with maps, plans, various primary sources and scraps of secondary text. This layout and approach may well be a source of learning difficulty. This does not, of course, mean that the use of varied sources should be terminated. Their value for developing historical and literary skills is too important for that. What it does mean is that we need to look very carefully at what is needed to make their usage effective.

Teachers' and Pupils' Views on the Difficulties of Studying History

The many dimensions to the issue of differentiation in History, and the dearth of evidence on these dimensions led to my decision to explore pupils' views on the subject, on what they saw as being needed to perform well in it, on what they saw as difficult about it and on what they found most helpful.[17] The research was based in a large city comprehensive school (with a very mixed catchment) and its main associated primary. Six boys and six girls from each of the years Primary 7, Secondary 1, Secondary 2 and Secondary 4 were interviewed: these pupils were teacher-selected to include lower, middle and upper abilities. Interviewing was extensive; pupil answers were taped and subsequently transcribed.

When asked 'what do you need to be good at to do History?' there was a noticeable tendency for pupils to speak first about language skills as crucial. As pupils matured and as Standard Grade had its impact, a growing awareness of the importance of source evaluating emerged, for example: 'You've got to work out whether it's biased and who wrote it and whether it's an eye witness or not'.

Examiners commonly comment on the problems pupils have with source evaluating, yet several pupils saw it as easier than the assessable element on knowledge and understanding because, as one put it: 'It's easier with a source to look at to help you'.

The burden of memorising material meant pupils view this latter element with unease even when their performance in tests suggested otherwise, for example, 'I find knowledge and understanding harder but always seem to get higher marks for it'.

Even at Standard Grade, History's language-based character provoked comment, for example, 'If you don't understand the source then you're not going to get any marks for the questions'.

History teachers would seem to have little choice about being language teachers too, yet interviews with the teachers involved produced an overwhelming focus on evaluating skills and a view that came close to suggesting these skills were so demanding as to be beyond some pupils, for example: 'When you come to evaluating it's actually very difficult to work out strategies how to help pupils. Pupils find it very difficult to know how to improve. They're not able to improve because basically they can't'.

Pupils were asked what they saw as being difficult about History. Primary 7 pupils simply dealt with the types of task they were set, observing that family trees were difficult and (not unreasonably), 'a worksheet is hard when some books don't have any information'.

References to difficulties in understanding a topic appeared at all levels of secondary school responses and were seen as being due to a variety of factors including a lack of interest in a topic, the complexity of the topic, and insufficient explanation by the teacher. The Industrial Revolution (Secondary 2) and the Russian Revolution (Secondary 4) attracted particular comment as being complex and confusing and with source materials that it was not easy to understand. As one able Secondary 4 pupil observed, it was hard to follow 'all the different parties. It's hard to keep track of the Provisional Government and the Soviets and the Bolsheviks. I'm all confused. We're moving through this booklet quite fast and it's not explained'.

The central importance of clear explanations of the historical past, of sources, and of tasks was abundantly evident in pupils' responses. It bears out work comparing differentiation strategies in English and Mathematics teaching that shows sensitivity to pupil needs and the ability to respond effectively are very highly valued: 'It's just the way he explains everything without making you sound stupid'.[18]

Skill in providing explanations, both as informal support as well as during initial clarification of what was expected from them, was seen by pupils as of more value in supporting their work than carefully prepared differentiated task sheets provided in their Mathematics lessons. The attributes of effective explanations have been very helpfully analysed and exemplified in a Leverhulme Primary Project publication.[19]

The Primary 7 teacher and the History staff teaching the pupils who were interviewed, all appreciated that contexts that had been personalised rather than left at an abstract level were more readily understood by pupils. The personalising of the past is a strategy recommended by Egan for pupils within this age span, pupils whom he sees as being at a 'romantic' stage when the 'otherness' of the past has a strong appeal. He exemplifies his view through a topic on the Industrial Revolution which he sees as best approached through the story of a dramatic figure like Brunel. However, the teachers using this topic at Secondary 2 seemed to be driven in directions shaped by readily available resources pitched at a somewhat confusing and rather abstract level that led them to conclude: 'the actual idea of something called an Industrial Revolution . . . some of the poorer ones find that difficult to grasp'.

Language issues loomed large in teacher's views too, for example, for Secondary 1 and 2: 'anything where there is written material that they have to read and take in and then present it in a written form, they do struggle'. By Standard Grade teachers saw the language of historical sources as a barrier to understanding because of 'words that are not commonly used . . . they can see the event and understand the event but the language is almost preventing them from seeing it'.

Pupils were asked if they thought that their study of History became more demanding as they progressed from Primary 7 to Secondary 4. A clear majority believed this to be so, explaining their views in terms of the amount of reading and writing expected, the complexity of topics, and ways of working. In Primary 7, one pupil explained you 'got to watch more programmes in Primary instead of looking up books all the time. You do more writing in Secondary'.

The minority of pupils who were not convinced that work had become harder included Secondary 1 and 2 pupils who stated: 'I find it easier in secondary because we have already done some of the stuff in Primary, for example, World War Two and Culloden'.

Secondary 4 pupils could see their work demanded a grasp of more complex historical issues, indeed one pupil complained the upward step from Secondary 2 to Secondary 3 was too steep, suggesting: 'Maybe it should have been a bit more difficult (in Secondary 2) because people like me thought it was easy. I was getting Grade 1 then and I did Standard Grade and my grades just fell'.

Pupils were asked what they found helpful in terms of ways of working, resources, and topics whose intrinsic interest was motivating. Their responses provide a very varied picture: some, for example, enjoyed working in groups and others preferred to work on their own. One Primary 7 pupil, though, expressed a considered view that: 'if you're doing research it's best to do it on your own. If you're doing a picture or a poster a pair is better. If you're making an object it's best to do it in a fairly big group'.

As pupils matured they appreciated the value of the detailed understanding provided by written text, though they remained highly critical of badly set-out, confused, and overcrowded pages of text and valued ways into such dense material, such as diagrams. It was not necessarily easy to separate out the different components of what pupils found helpful. All 12 Primary 7 pupils enjoyed their Victorian Times study, yet this view seemed strongly influenced by the fieldwork and visits they engaged in and the role play they enacted in class time. Secondary 1 and 2 pupils rated their World War Two topic as the most enjoyable but Exploration and Discovery, and the Industrial Revolution as the ones that they liked least. Standard Grade pupils rated World War One as the most interesting: neither of the other two topics aroused significant enthusiasm at this level.

Positive dislike of topics reflected a mix of personal interest, the intelligibility of resources and the level of abstraction of the topic. A number of pupils expressed real hostility to 'The History Detective' ('it's just pictures and answering questions. I like things more when you have to look up in books and videos'), Skara Brae (denounced as tedious in content and tasks) and Industrial Britain ('I thought it was hard'). Within the pupil responses can be seen one of the problems of differentiation, for there were also pupils who denounced what they had to do as insufficiently challenging (for example, the Industrial Revolution 'The questions were easy, you just take in stuff and repeat it back in a different way') whilst welcoming the ideas and issues of a difficult topic like the Russian Revolution which offered insights into: 'the uprising of the whole thing. How a country can swing from being governed by a dictator to the complete opposite and be run by revolutionaries'.

These varied responses provide a vivid account of a real problem, for mixed ability classes need topics, resources, tasks and forms of support that challenge able pupils interested in ideas, and yet must also provide effectively for pupils easily deterred by these very matters. In so far as a differentiation strategy was in place in the secondary school concerned it took the form of open-ended questions in Secondary 1 and 2, allowing differentiation by outcome – and some core and extension work in Secondary 3 and 4 – with all the attendant problems. One pupil noted: 'It's invariably the Credit people who finish the booklet first, so we're told to do extensions while the rest of the class catches up'.

Thus able pupils reinforce their learning whilst their less able colleagues gasp along, constantly confronted by new work. The core and extension strategy would seem to have inspectorate approval yet pupils coming to a topic do not start from the same place – the difference in reading ages alone is a vital factor – and aiming to satisfy all with common material risks baffling the least able and boring the most able. Despair shines through the comment of one Secondary 4 pupil: 'Some folk are General/Credit and some are General/Foundation but we're all doing Credit work. I didn't understand the Credit work . . . we haven't used the Foundation Revision Guide just the General/Credit Guide because most of the class is General/Credit'.

A Differentiated Task – A Secondary 1 Experiment

In a second research project it was decided to focus on just one element in the complex range of dimensions shaping differentiation in the learning and teaching of History. This research was carried out with 10 members of a Secondary 1 class coming to the end of their first year in a city comprehensive school with a significantly middle-class catchment. Pupils had been studying the medieval period and it was decided to use one dimension of the period as a focus for work. The chosen dimension – attacking a castle – had been studied in outline: a small pack of resources was put together on this topic that consisted of a task sheet, an information sheet on castles, pictures and written descriptions of siege machines, and accounts of three different sieges, each of which used a different strategy.

Two quite different tasks were devised, each dealing with besieging a castle and each drawing upon the same pool of resources:

Task A

During the Middle Ages those who became knights were expected to be expert warriors. One of the things they had to learn about was how to capture castles. Imagine you have been asked to write a manual or handbook entitled *How to Besiege a Castle* to guide one of these warriors.

Task B

Imagine you are an historian. You have been asked to help write a book entitled *Castles* for people who know very little about History. You have to write the chapter on 'Besieging Castles'.

This study formed but a small part of a major research project directed by language experts that explored the very pervasive activity of writing tasks undertaken in response to reading. It was recognised that: 'the practice of History centres on the discovery, interpretation and collation of information from sources. . . . we aimed to have pupils extract information from within texts, to have them arrange the selected information in some kind of logical sequence, and to have them construct their own text'.[20]

The study stressed the centrality of language issues. This whole language dimension offers a very rewarding area for History teachers to explore, helped perhaps, by appropriate inservice. There are detailed studies of the issue [21] and the author has outlined some of its dimensions in two articles.[22] However, the tasks were also intended to shed light on pupils' awareness of History too. The task could point the way to a particular strategy for differentiation that would begin by setting tasks that varied the challenges offered to pupils but did so within a common content area, drawing upon a common pool of resources. In some schools the implementation of Standard Grade Investigations has used this strategy, providing teachers with experience in implementing differentiation in a way that avoids the problems of the core and extension approach.

The two tasks differed in difficulty since Task A consisted essentially of description, which, like the narrative form, provides pupils with a straightforward type of text to create. Moreover, many of the items from which pupils derived their responses required but limited modification in order to result in an appropriate form. Task B, however, posed the more demanding challenge of creating expository text as well as requiring a greater degree of genre-transformation. It also provided a test of the pupils' ability to undertake a task testing skills-based History's ultimate purpose. Pupils commonly undertake a 'What is History?' unit (as these pupils had done) and are expected to apply their understanding in subsequent work. They study specific sources, consider factors which shape their value to an historian, and compare an historian to a detective. However, what historians do, above all, is create general text from their researches into specific sources: pupils may meet such texts in their studies, commonly in school textbook form at this level, but eventually, in Secondary 5 and 6, in the works of professional academic historians. What pupils lack at present is an effective linkage between the two dimensions of source study and text creation. Visitors to the Viking 'Jorvik' Centre in York observe and learn about the Viking way of life. They are then allowed the opportunity of studying specific items of evidence on which these general conclusions are based. At present school History teachers lack carefully worked equivalents showing general text to pupils, then showing the evidence and the interpretation of evidence on which such text is based. It may be that lack of work in this area contributes to pupils' uncertainties when faced with secondary text items and their tendency on the one hand simply to accept such items as truths, and on the other hand to take them as 'less valuable' than primary source items. The CHATA project has probed the issue, offering pupils two different stories about the same historical topic then questioning pupils as to why these stories differ and sorting responses into a differentiated list – providing insights into pupils' appreciation of how historical text is created.[23]

Task A responses showed pupils had a good grasp of the audience for whom they were writing and were able to provide direct guidance, for example: 'If you want to besiege a castle you must know some important facts about it, such as if it's made of wood or stone and if it has any roads nearby . . .' And: 'If the castle that you want to besiege is made of wood or has wooden foundations then the best way to capture it is by using fire or by battering the walls down. Good pieces of equipment to consider for this are battering rams and ballistas for making holes, and burning arrows for setting fire to the castle'.

Information was clearly organised, usually in a list of tactics to be tried; if the first in the sequence failed, then others were offered as possible approaches.

Task B posed more problems; two of the five pupils attempting this task were able to rise to the challenge and produce organised and relevant text from the descriptions and narratives that they were using. The remaining three pupils were unable to achieve the necessary level of generality and, instead, provided summary accounts of each of the three sieges offered them in the source pack. Even when an account began in general terms, it soon moved to the specific, for example: 'Throughout History there have been many castles built, most have been broken into. In this chapter you will find out about the methods and tactics used to besiege a castle.

Even the most secure castles can be broken into or taken because the defending soldiers have been starved out.

One castle 2½ miles outside London had walls over 100 feet high and 12 feet thick. The walls were battered with siege engines without any success . . .' (An account of this Siege followed).

It may well be that asking pupils to create general statements of real worth from sources that deal with specific situations is a very high level task indeed.

Conclusion

This study illustrates the tangled inter-mixture of language issues and historical issues that endlessly confront teachers when seeking to provide for pupils' needs. Far more classroom-based research is required, as well as vigorous exploration of what the specialists in other subject areas that we draw upon for History would reasonably expect at particular stages. (Analysis of maps or statistical data are two very obvious examples here). If official expectations for meeting individual pupil needs are to be properly met then effective support, with strategies of proven success are required. The coming of Higher Still and suggestions for accelerated learning from Secondary 1 serve to add to this need. Soundly-based model strategies are urgently needed.

Notes

1. Amy Stewart Fraser, *The Hills of Home*, (London, 1973), p.104.

2. W. Gordon Lawrence (ed.) *Roots in a Northern Landscape*, (Edinburgh, 1996), p.60.

3. A useful survey is provided in J. Appleby, L. Hunt and M. Jacob, *Telling the Truth About History*, (New York, 1994).

4. M. Phillips, *The Observer*, 30/10/1994.

5. Effective Learning and Teaching in Scottish Secondary Schools, Scottish Office Education Department, 1992, p.31.

6. Quoted in M. Simpson, *Differentiation and Research*, (Aberdeen, 1994), p. 10.

7. Peter John, 'Academic Tasks in History Classrooms' in *Research in Education*, (1994), p.51.

8. For example see research on group work such as K. Wheldall, M. Morris and P. Vaughan, 'Rows versus Tables' in *Educational Psychology 1*, (1981), showing group work producing significantly less task-focused behaviour.

9. M. Booth, 'Students' Historical Thinking and the History of the National Curriculum in England' in *Theory and Research on Social Education*, No. 21, 1993.

10. K. Egan, *Individual Development in the Curriculum*, (London, 1986).

11. See, for example, A. Dickinson, P. Lee, and R. Ashby, Research Methods and some Findings on Rational Understanding' in A. Pendry and C. O'Neill (eds.) *Principles and Practice*, (Lancaster, 1997), p.113–123.

12. Environmental Studies 5–14, Scottish Office Education Department, 1993, p.35–36.

13. S.J. Thornton and R. Vukelich, 'Effects of Children's Understanding of Time Concepts on Historical Understanding' in *Theory and Research in Social Education*, (Winter, 1988), p.79.

14. S.S. Wineburg, 'Historical Problem-Solving: A Study of the Cognitive Processes used in the Evaluation of Documentary and Pictorial Evidence' in *The Journal of Educational Psychology*, Vol. 83, 1991, p.84.

15. M.T. Downey and L.S. Levstik, 'Teaching and Learning History: The Research Base', *Social Education*, 1988, p.341.

16. P. Schrag, The Emasculated Voice of the Textbook, *Saturday Review*, January 1967.

17. Sydney Wood and Fran Payne, 'Issues of Learning Difficulty and Differentiation in History: A Comparison of Pupil and Teacher Views', (Aberdeen, 1995). (Unpublished research report).

18. M. Simpson and J. Ure, *What's the Difference? A Study of Differentiation in Scottish Secondary Schools*, (Aberdeen, 1993), p.57.

19. E.K. Wragg and G. Brown, *Explaining*, (London, 1993).

20. R. Fyfe, G. Lewis, E. Mitchell, 'Developing Pupil Competence in Reading to Write'. (Unpublished report to the Scottish Office Education Department).

21. See, for example, E. Lunzer and K. Gardner, *Learning from the Written Word*, (Edinburgh, 1984).

22. S.H. Wood, 'Understanding the Past' in *Language and Learning*, October 1995 and 'Writing Up the Past' in *Language and Learning*, December 1995.

23. See, Peter Lee, 'A Lot of Guesswork Goes On. Children's Understanding of Historical Accounts', *Teaching History*, 92, 1998.

8

Syllabus Design – A National or World View?

David Duncan

History Education in Global Perspective

The place of History or History education in the school curriculum is a frequently revisited issue in many countries around the world. The reasons for this are not difficult to find: politicians and educationists alike are aware of the critical role History can play in influencing individual and national consciousness, in developing a sense of identity (for good or ill), and for shaping the sort of society which they feel is desirable. One consequence of this is that History is accorded a key place in the learning experiences offered to young people in most countries; a second is that the content of History education is often contested terrain, discussed, debated and sometimes fought over by those inside and outside the education community. This is a not unreasonable state of affairs, and it seems unlikely that the awareness of the potential role of History and its consequences will alter much in the foreseeable future.

Of course, the nature of the History education offered in different countries varies greatly, depending on the nature of the society and its education system. Nationalistic regimes in diverse parts of the world tend to insist that History education in schools is about the making of the nation – their nation, and the struggles of the people to establish, defend and glorify the country. Legends and icons are given precedence and patriotism overtly encouraged through an emphasis on the suffering, heroism and genius embedded in the country's past. Thus, in South Africa under *apartheid*, even African children were required to study the deeds of the Voortrekkers, the struggles of the Afrikaner *volk* against British imperialism and the remarkable achievements of the South African economy in the 20th century. The most commonly used textbook – written by a member of the Broederbond and published by a printer with close ties to the ruling party – treated the rise of Nazi Germany in only mildly critical terms and illustrated the period with two pictures – one of a brooding Hitler, sub-titled 'author of *Mein Kampf*', and the other of German troops marching victoriously through a conquered city.

However, nationalistic regimes are not the only ones to seek to develop young people's understanding of their own country's past. In some instances, a national curriculum is laid down which all children are expected to follow during the compulsory years of schooling; this may include defined content, specifying historical periods, topics and events which must be covered, and experiences which all young people should have – such as a visit to a national museum or historical site. In other countries, teachers are guided in terms of content via national advice, or through standard textbooks which may be subsidised or approved by national agencies. In others still, local or regional bodies control the content of the curriculum, while a minority of states leave issues of content entirely up to the good judgement of teachers.

For the most part, though, it is accepted that young people must be encouraged to develop an understanding of the society of which they are a part. History education is seen as essential to this aspect of learning, and some definition of the content of the curriculum is justified in terms of equality of experience and balance. In many continental European countries, the place of History in the school curriculum is bound up with the importance accorded to Civics education. This multi-disciplinary pursuit seeks to ensure that young people are equipped with the knowledge, skills and values required to be a good citizen. It involves an understanding of the past as well as of the present; it requires a familiarity with the law and with the rights and responsibilities of individuals in a democratic society. Civics education attracts considerable support from international organisations such as the European Union, UNESCO and the Council of Europe.[1] It is, not surprisingly, a major issue in many eastern European countries which are seeking to forge new education systems and new societies which are no longer dominated by Marxist dogma.[2] European educationists are often mildly taken aback by the British lack of familiarity with the term 'Civics'; they see its absence as an oversight or deficiency which is ripe for correction.

Whereas national History enjoys a comfortable place in the education systems of most countries, the years since World War II have seen a much greater emphasis on nurturing the virtues of tolerance, mutual understanding and respect. In our own continent, the great political project of the post-war period – the foundation and evolution of the Common Market/European Community/European Union – has given both a purpose and an impetus to this endeavour. While some member states have jealously guarded national control of their education systems, all Ministers of Education signed up for a 1988 agreement to give 'the European Dimension' a structural position within the school curriculum. As an early document published by the Consortium of Institutions for Development and Research in Education in Europe (CIDREE) noted, this was based on the perceived need to provide young people with the knowledge, skills and insights necessary to function as 'effective European citizens'. In reality, the initiative had a clear political aim, namely to promote collaboration and integration among European countries by exploring:

(1) European collaborative organisations
(2) Reasons for collaboration and integration in Europe
(3) The future of collaboration and integration in Europe
(4) Consequences of future collaboration and integration for citizens.[3]

History (along with other subjects) was seen as an important contributor to this aspect of Civics education; it could be used to draw young people's attention to the disasters and mistakes of the past, as well as to imply a trend towards more desirable and worthwhile international undertakings.

In terms of the overall 'global perspective' on History education, the subject is accorded a highly significant place in most countries' education systems. It is generally seen as having a particular part to play in developing specific knowledge, skills and values. The place accorded to local or regional, national and international History varies in different corners of the globe; here in Europe, national History remains important, but the inclusion of a European perspective has been purposefully nurtured by the EU and other international organisations. The UK is unusual (in this continent at least) in not having a recognisable component called Civics education in the school curriculum. But that does not mean that these issues are not being addressed in Scotland and the other 'home countries', in these days of rapid political and constitutional change.

The Scottish Answer to the Debate

For some observers, the past couple of decades have not been kind to the study of History in Scottish schools. As the curriculum has developed, History as a discrete subject has been squeezed. More time has had to be devoted to new areas of learning such as information technology, and other subjects have acquired a new sense of urgency – for example, Modern Languages in the primary school, or Personal and Social Education for older pupils. At the same time, the notion of integrating History education with Geography and Modern Studies has gained ground, especially in Secondary 1 and Secondary 2, where pressure on time and the need to reduce the number of teachers encountered by pupils has brought added strains.

Meanwhile, History has, for some, been kidnapped by new teaching methods which emphasise how learning takes place over what is learned. Taken to its logical conclusion, this line of thought assumes that the content of History education is not at all important – so long as young people are learning the skills of the historian, and provided that they are equipping themselves with an understanding of how the historian goes about his or her craft, there really is no need to fill empty heads with useless and soon-to-be-forgotten knowledge. In the post-modern age, this argument has been given a new lease of life, as media-wise teachers have sought to ensure that pupils are not lead astray by historians who feign objectivity but in fact peddle a particular line or argument. Deconstructing the text has become a key skill, while acquisition of 'facts' can be covered by knowing where to look – and then judging whether to believe what you read.

Such is the pessimist's view of History's plight in Scottish schools over the past years. Its purveyors point to the decline in the numbers taking History after Secondary 2, and to the battle to retain its toehold of teaching time at the primary and early secondary stages. A conspiracy is suspected, whereby History will eventually be wiped from the curriculum, to make way for more socially relevant pass-times such as parenting classes or core skills development. The dreich landscape looks all the worse when viewed from the sun-kissed valleys of continental Europe, where History is believed to live a charmed existence, safe from the most short-sighted of time-tablers.

On the other hand, there are signs that the worst fears of historians may be exaggerated. History education in Scottish schools is taught in far more interesting and innovative ways than it was 20 or 30 years ago. Teachers in Primary and Secondary schools make use of a wide range of methodologies and resources, including new technology based materials such as CD-ROMs and web sites; they seek to develop the investigative and enquiry skills of young people through project or assignment work; and they access a wealth of primary source material which archives and libraries are increasingly eager to make available.

Developments at policy level are also providing opportunities to strengthen the place of History education in the primary and secondary curriculum. The re-working of courses at Secondary 5 and Secondary 6 as part of the Higher Still Development Programme has been relatively un-contentious in the field of History: as part of the official support for the programme, a range of writers have been commissioned to address identified resource needs. Other materials will also be developed as commercial publishers, teacher education institutions and others concentrate their efforts on producing the more substantial resources which generally follow major development initiatives. Meanwhile at Standard Grade, while the abandonment of the 'investigation' component of the Secondary 3/Secondary 4 course was felt by some to be regrettable, it may be that the new course will be regarded as less demanding by pupils, and therefore more attractive as part of a diet of seven or eight Standard Grades.

The recent review by the Scottish Consultative Council on the Curriculum (SCCC) of the place of Scottish History in the curriculum helped to provoke a debate about the place of History education as a whole in Scottish schools. On the back of this, the public are perhaps a little better informed about the good work which is going on in schools in this area; policy makers are possibly more conscious of the value of History in the curriculum; and further impetus has been given to the generation of resources by a spectrum of public sector and commercial providers.

Also significant is the fact that constitutional change in the form of the Scottish Parliament and the strengthening of European institutions is gradually giving rise to a debate about the relationship between the school curriculum and citizenship. Although a dedicated course on Civics education on the European model is unlikely to find a place in the crowded Scottish curriculum, educationists are beginning to consider the role which various subjects and areas of the curriculum can play in promoting 'education for citizenship'. Chief among these, surely, are Modern Studies, Personal and Social Education and History. As the SCCC's Government-endorsed *Position Statement on Scottish History in the Curriculum* identified:

> Scottish History is important for its role in fostering informed, responsible and active citizenship. The informed citizen living in Scotland requires a knowledge of Scottish History in order to understand how the present society has evolved and to place it in the wider British, European and global contexts.
>
> Citizenship in its widest sense involves choices and decisions on many different matters. The study of History, involving as it does the analysis of evidence and judgements about the relevance of information, enables the responsible citizen to make the best choices for the future of Scotland.[4]

The study of History can contribute to education for citizenship, not only by developing young people's understanding of society, but also by nurturing a sense of belonging in the local, national and international senses. A key strand of the work of the SCCC over the past decade has been the development of guidance for schools on values in education, and the central importance of creating a positive climate or ethos.[5] In successive documents, a core set of values which Council believes schools should seek to promote are articulated; these cover respect for self, respect and caring for others; a sense of social responsibility; a commitment to learning; and, significantly, a sense of belonging.[6] A primary function of the school should be to create a climate for learning by exemplifying these values within the life of the school; in doing so, pupils and teachers will naturally be encouraged to feel a sense of belonging towards the school itself as a community.

At the same time, however, it may be argued that individual subjects have something to contribute to the development of a child's sense of belonging. The study of the past provides a valuable opportunity for children to explore their own sense of belonging to a local, national and international community. In the process, young people are afforded the chance to consider the meaning of such complex concepts as community and citizenship, rights and responsibilities, and moral and immoral actions.

Given the emphasis which has been placed in Scotland on issues of ethos and which is likely to be devoted to the relationship between education and citizenship, it seems reasonable to conclude that for Scotland, History should have a crucial place in the school curriculum, for much the same reasons as it does in most other countries. History is vital not merely for what it teaches us about the past and present, but for its contribution to the development of young people as well-rounded, responsible individuals with a strong sense of belonging to a wider, inclusive community.

Breadth and Balance

One of the features of the debate about History education in Scotland over the last few decades has been a shift in what educationists feel it is important for young people to learn. Like many educational debates, different arguments have come in and out of fashion, with long-discarded notions being resurrected in new guises at various points and presented as brilliant critiques of contemporary thinking. In the last few years, we have, at last, seen the abandonment of what was essentially a sterile debate about whether content was more important than skills, or vice versa. It is now generally accepted that both content and skills are worth debating, and that considerations of what is taught should co-exist with research and reflection on how this area of the curriculum is addressed. Within the content debate, there is, moreover, a widespread if not universal acceptance that young people should not merely be treated to excerpts from History, but that an effort should be made to encourage pupils to build up a 'mental map' of the past as a whole (a phrase borrowed from work undertaken by the Curriculum and Assessment Authority for Wales). This does not mean that every period of History has to be covered in detail, but it does require that Primary and Secondary Schools make every effort to ensure a balance of coverage, and that topics are contextualised to facilitate some understanding of the wider picture.

In terms of content, we have seen some movement in the type of History taught in the classroom. Fifty years ago, school History was generally the politics of the past – there was an excessive concentration on great men, with a good deal of attention paid to kings and queens for the medieval and early modern periods, and a focus on constitutional change and governments for the later period. International History concerned an interminable series of alliances and conflicts in Europe, plus the growth of the British Empire. In more recent times, the pendulum has swung toward a much greater stress on social History, taking into account the lives of ordinary people and requiring an understanding of what it was like to live in different times and different circumstances.

Welcome as this move is in many respects, there remains a worry that the History taught in Scottish schools still lacks an essential balance between political, economic, social and cultural dimensions. Social History can really only be meaningful where it is studied as one aspect of the past; taken in isolation (as there is a tendency to do in some Primary classrooms), divorced from an appreciation of systems of government, religion, art, thought and economic structures and processes and – critically – how these changed or did not change over time – it cannot provide the sorts of insights which History education ought to offer to young people.

Balance in the History taught in schools is equally important in terms of the geographical area of study. The SCCC's Review of Scottish History in the Curriculum addressed this issue in common-sense terms, calling for roughly equal amounts of time to be devoted to the local, Scottish, British, European and global spheres. This means that some 40 per cent of the History taught is Scottish, but allows the focus on the local area which many schools have developed strongly over recent years. More importantly, though, *Scottish History in the Curriculum* argued that children should be encouraged to see the links between the different spheres. Thus, the Scottish contribution to the growth of the British Empire might be explored, or Scottish examples of Renaissance art and architecture examined; the Scottish experience of World War II could be considered, or the impact of globalisation on life in twentieth-century Scotland debated.

From another viewpoint, balance in terms of geographical area should also require schools to consider globally important topics regardless of their impact on or relationship with Scotland's past. For example, ancient civilisations, the French Revolution, the Russian Revolution, World War II and the rise of the USA to sole superpower status may be regarded as of such significance that young people ought to have the opportunity to study them at some stage before the end of Secondary 2. Likewise, there is a strong case for exploring some aspect of the developing world – possibly through a case study – to foster an appreciation of global History in its truest sense, and an understanding of the world as it is today.

The study of Scottish History – the national view – should not be treated as a pretext for inculcating a nationalistic or ethnocentric tendency in young people. It is vital that children are exposed to the History of other countries and other peoples on the basis of the local/Scottish/British/European/World division described above. This encourages children to see Scottish achievements in perspective, and to recognise that, in many areas, the high points of other nations far surpass those of our own.

However, in order to acquire a fair understanding of the past, it is also necessary for children to explore the more difficult aspects of Scotland's History. For example, it is sad that some teachers still shy away from studying the Reformation, for fear of tackling issues likely to inflame the immature passions of their pupils. At another level, topics such as the Enlightenment are neglected, partly because they are felt to be too challenging for pupils in Primary and early Secondary. There is a case for arguing that such contentious and complex topics should be made accessible to young people through sound resources, careful planning and good teaching. Similarly, aspects of Scotland's past which may be regarded as shameful – for example, the torture and execution of witches at a time when other parts of Europe were abandoning such barbaric practices; the part played by Scotsmen in the Atlantic slave trade of the eighteenth century, or the sectarianism which marred life in the towns and cities for much of the nineteenth and twentieth centuries – should be examined, if only to show that Scotland is not free of the sort of racism and oppression which afflicts some parts of the world today.

To enshrine breadth and balance as the cornerstones of the History curriculum on the basis of 40 or so hours of teaching time a year is a near-impossible task. The range of factors which a teacher can reasonably be expected to keep in mind has to be limited if the advice offered is to be helpful rather than burdensome. Moreover, it is essential that teachers are afforded at least some freedom to explore their own interests and enthusiasms, and to encourage children to investigate topics which capture their imagination. Even so, issues of content do matter, not only to educationists, but to society as a whole. In order to ensure that the available time is used to best effect, and to meet the requirements of breadth and balance, the political/economic/social/cultural formula, coupled with the local/national/Scottish/British/European/global division, should provide a sound basis for the selection of content. The need to address the less heroic episodes in Scotland's past is also worthy of debate as programmes of study are compiled.

Coherence across the Curriculum

As Jim McGonigle notes in Chapter 12 of this volume there is an ongoing debate in Scotland on the possibility of integrating History education with Geography and the study of society at the Primary and early Secondary stages. This notion generates considerable passion amongst historians, some of whom regard it as the death knell of the subject. History, it is argued, permits the development of a discrete set of knowledge, skills and dispositions; its combination with other subjects, which possess their own rationales within the curriculum, would lead to an unacceptable mish mash. Moreover, the professional skills of History graduates are clearly distinct from those of Geographers, Political Scientists or Sociologists; History teachers could no more do justice to the school subjects related to these disciplines than they could deliver an effective course in Mathematics or Latin. The argument is therefore made that, while a degree of integration is permissible at the primary stages, by secondary, young people are best taught by bespoke historians and their counterparts in other subject disciplines.

Behind this argument lurks a whole host of considerations, not the least of which relate to the current promotion structure, questions of time-tabling flexibility and time constraints. There is also a concern that, in order for young people to make informed subject choices at the end of Secondary 2, they ought to have had at least some familiarity with the subject they are selecting for Standard Grade. These contentions have some validity; it would be inappropriate to lay down a strict set of guidelines which required, for example, full integration of social subjects for all pupils in the first two years of secondary school.

On the other hand, the world of historical scholarship and practice does suggest that the best History is written where authors take full account of the insights of other disciplines. For example, the flowering of the History workshop phenomenon in England or the development of the *annales* school in France, owed much to individuals who opened their minds to other academic skills in the fields of Sociology, Economics and Statistics. To put it more pejoratively, where historians shut themselves off from other disciplines and regard themselves as having nothing to learn from colleagues, their outputs are often dry and uninspiring. The implications of this for the Secondary School curriculum is surely that children should be encouraged to see the links between History and other subjects, not necessarily through fully integrated courses, but via a carefully planned curriculum which seeks to apply the skills learnt in one subject to the content of another. Just as computational skills can be applied to historical topics, so an historical perspective can help to illuminate human and physical Geography; similarly, few would disagree that today's society has to be put into historical perspective in order to understand it, while an appreciation of the principles of economics can shed new light on say, the industrial revolution. For these reasons – quite apart from the other arguments for subject integration at Secondary 1/ Secondary 2 – it makes sense to ensure a coherent programme of study which embraces all the social subjects and other disciplines too. The best historical scholarship may not always be accessible to pupil and teacher, but we should at least seek to learn from developments in academia as we take forward curriculum development and planning.

Politics and Culture

Any consideration of the way in which History education features in the school curriculum must take account of current trends in society as a whole. In Scotland, it happens that these developments are particularly dramatic at the present time, involving as they do the establishment of a devolved Parliament responsible for many areas of public life. There are other changes which should also be considered, including the advent of a pan-European currency, the strengthening of European institutions of government, the alterations to the constitution at UK level and, within Scotland, the apparent growth in support for outright independence.

In cultural terms, it may be argued that the Scots are more self-confident than they used to be, more inclined to recognise the contributions that Scotland can make on the international stage. This is not to say that Scotland is becoming more insular: on the contrary, there is perhaps a greater appreciation today of the way in which indigenous Scottish manifestations of culture measure up to those from other countries, of the interplay between cultures, and of the contribution of cultural borrowings to lifestyle. This broadening understanding is underpinned by huge numbers who now travel overseas on a fairly regular basis and by the attractiveness of Scotland as a tourist destination. Foreign investment in Scotland and a renewed willingness by Scottish-based companies to invest overseas may further bind life in Scotland to a global community and increase Scottish public awareness of the need to be internationally minded.

History education in Primary and early Secondary should seek to ensure that young people have access to the historical background to all these developments. Pupils should be made aware of the story of Scotland's relations with England, the union of the crowns and parliaments, and of the reasons for the re-establishment of a parliament in 1999. The background to the European Union and the opposing arguments for and against, should not be left to the Modern Studies teacher, but should be treated with due attention to its historical roots and development. Changes to the Scottish economy over time – its place as part of the workshop of the world in the eighteenth and nineteenth centuries, and the transformations it has undergone in the twentieth century – should be explored as part of an historical continuum. And the highpoints of Scotland's cultural History, including its links with developments in European culture, should be explored, not merely from an art and design perspective, but with an eye to the historical relationship between culture and society.

The substance of the argument here is that History education should take both a national and a global perspective in reflecting the course of current political, social cultural and economic developments. History should not be studied merely for its own sake, but in order to equip the citizens of tomorrow with an understanding of the world around them, as it is today and as it is likely to develop in the future. Of course, this should not mean that we limit our attentions to the very recent past, nor should we encourage children to believe that there is an inevitability about the way events unfold over time. Human progress is messy and uneven; it would be wrong to try to impose an order or clarity on events which are fundamentally confused or inexplicable. Even so, young people should be asked to recognise that History education has a practical utility and purpose. Most important of all, they should be encouraged to discover for themselves how the study of the past can illuminate present-day circumstances. This process is best taken forward where children learn about the country in which they are living, as well as learning about and from other peoples and countries in the UK, Europe and the world.

Conclusion

History education is regarded as a vital part of the curriculum in most parts of the world. In many countries, it is seen as playing a crucial role in relation to Civics education, or education for citizenship. In Scotland, the debate on citizenship and how it is treated in the curriculum is only now beginning to get underway, but the values which should underpin citizenship education are well defined and are generally accepted. The study of History can and should support the nurturing of certain values, including respect for self, respect for others and, crucially, a sense of belonging. A balance of content based on local, Scottish, British, European and world themes provides appropriate contexts for developing these values, as well as ensuring that the History studied in schools is neither parochial nor nationalistic.

While the content of History education in schools is now regarded as a legitimate topic for debate, there is no single agreed formula; schools should continue to make their own selections in line with local needs and their own professional judgements. The important points are that the History curriculum is broad and balanced, that it coheres with what is being studied in other areas or subjects, and that young people are encouraged to appreciate the relevance of skills developed elsewhere to the study of the past.

Likewise, the relevance of History to present-day developments should not be lost on those studying it, and young people's understanding of the links between Scottish History and the History of other parts of the world should be nurtured. In learning from and about other countries, young people might also be afforded the opportunity to learn with others. The Internet and the World Wide Web, to say nothing of sound and video links, may provide the means to compare the perspectives of young people in different parts of the globe as they investigate the same historical subject matter. As we move into a new millennium, it may be that we can learn together from the mistakes of the past, as much as from the fast-changing technologies of the future.

Notes

1. Council for Cultural Co-operation Project: Education for Democratic Citizenship: A document-based Report on Council of Europe Projects 1989–1998 – outline. Council of Europe, Strasbourg, 1998.

   Council for Cultural Co-operation Project: Learning and Teaching about the History of Europe in the Twentieth Century – Second Meeting of the Project Group – Meeting Report. Council of Europe, Strasbourg, 1998.

2. The State of History Education in Europe: Challenges and Implications of the 'Youth and History' Survey. Hamburg, 1998.

3. Geography and History with a European Dimension: Manual for Teachers in Secondary Education. CIDREE, Enschede, 1992, p. 15.

4. Scottish History in the Curriculum: A Statement of Position from the Scottish Consultative Council on the Curriculum. Scottish Consultative Council on the Curriculum, Dundee, 1998.

5. The Heart of the Matter: A Paper for Discussion and Development. Scottish Consultative Council on the Curriculum, Dundee, 1995.

6. Values in Education: A Scottish Consultative Council on the Curriculum Paper for Discussion and Development. Scottish Consultative Council on the Curriculum, Dundee, 1991.

9

Information and Communication Technology in History Education

Bob Munro

A Marriage Made in Heaven?

Information Technology (IT), as it was called until the mid-1990s, or Information and Communications Technology (ICT), the current term which encompasses the associated communications and computer networking facilities, has been an integral element in education for some 20 years. This period has been characterised by heavy and uncritical investment in the principal areas of hardware, software and training – particularly hardware – and a variable uptake and use of ICT by different subject disciplines and the different sectors of education. Unfortunately much of the investment went on rapidly obsolescent hardware and there was a general unwillingness to support the provision of adequate and appropriate software or training teachers in how best to exploit ICT resources. Despite these problems, ICT has grown in importance and the educational applications have expanded considerably. It is viewed as the key resource for education in the millennium – a resource which many maintain will transform learning and teaching.

From the earliest introduction of computers in schools Scottish History teachers have expressed interest in making use of this technology in their classrooms. Early and successful initiatives, such as the Census databases project in the former Strathclyde Region, provided valuable experiences and the prospect of a glittering future.[1] Indeed, in those early days the fusion of History and IT appeared to be a marriage made in heaven! History was a subject discipline replete with information, in so many forms, on so many topics. IT offered the possibility of unlimited and totally interconnected storage of information and technocrats promised sophisticated technology tools to aid analysis and interpretation of information. Significant but judicious adoption and integration of IT would surely shift learning and teaching in History into overdrive!

Sadly, despite the enthusiastic efforts of many History teachers over the past 20 years and an ever widening range of information and communication technology applications, ICT has only achieved limited adoption and has certainly not permeated or significantly contributed to the learning and teaching process of History in Scottish classrooms. Currently resourcing is limited, uptake is patchy and use is very irregular. However, many of the difficulties encountered by pioneer teachers have been resolved and the forces for change are massing.

There are strong grounds for a confident assertion that, by the turn of the millennium, most Scottish History teachers will embrace ICT enthusiastically and consequently their pupils will derive considerable benefits from opportunities to use ICT across the History curriculum. Used sensibly, sensitively and imaginatively ICT can expand historical knowledge, assist understanding of events and processes of the past, establish concepts and develop a wide range of History skills.

Past, Present and Future

Just how much has the History-ICT relationship changed over the past decade and what could happen in the near future?

If we strapped on a virtual reality headset and visited Clydeside Secondary in 1989 we would find a typically hard pressed History Department, coping with constant curricular change. The staff are John Glennie, a Principal Teacher of some 15 years' experience, and Ian Groves, a young graduate fresh from teacher training. Ian gained some experience of using computers during his teacher training and would really like to progressively build IT into classroom activities. In Room 21 the highly motivated pupils of class IA are busy, clustered in huddled groups, exploring a range of evidence about their Home Area (a general Social Subjects study in the school). Some are reading yellowed newspaper clippings, others shuffle prints, pictures and postcards, one group is viewing archive film and another is listening to the collected taped reminiscences of local worthies. In the nearby graveyard a small, trustworthy group are videotaping the Minister as he describes some of the more notable headstones.

Ian has yet to find a way of using the departmental computer resource to support this investigation of evidence – although he was recently inspired by *Using Graveyards and Cemeteries for Investigations*.[2]

The computer resource is next door, where Mr Glennie is discussing the 'Sarajevo Assassination' with 3A. Not that the computer plays any part in this activity – a BBC Model B, shared by all the Social Subjects departments, gathers dust on its trolley – a victim of limited software and staff indifference. Tight departmental budgets restricted John Glennie's software purchasing to three packages – *Viking England*, *Front Page Extra* and *Wagons West*.[3] *Viking England* was used successfully with first year classes but appears to have been damaged. *Front Page Extra* is used occasionally when a group has a report to create and *Wagons West* has been used only once. Ian found it took one group of pupils 40 minutes to 'travel the trail' across the American Rockies – and there are eight groups in most classes!

A decade on (21 March 1999) Clydeview Secondary is edging towards the millennium. The same staff inhabit the History department – older, wiser and both with a couple of computer-related in-service courses under their belts. Their new headteacher, appointed in 1997, is an ICT enthusiast who was instrumental in securing three Macintosh computers for Room 21 and one with a built-in CD-ROM drive for Room 22. The BBC lies forgotten in a corner of the staff base – its software used as coffee coasters. There is no floppy-disc software for the Macintoshes (so they are mainly used for word processing) although there are excellent CD-ROMs – *Grolier*; *Tiree, Famine and Clearance 1840–1900*; *Eyewitness History of the World*; *World of the Vikings* (a superb multimedia product bearing no comparison to the earlier BBC package) and *World War Two*.[4]

The brave new world of the connected society and access to the Internet, the World Wide Web (WWW) and the Scottish Virtual Teachers Centre, which staff are always reading about, is still six months away. Connection is promised in September 1999 to coincide with the national, in-depth, New Opportunities Fund training designed to ensure all teachers acquire the mandatory ICT competences recently drawn up by the Scottish Office Education and Industry Department (SOEID).

Forward now to explore 21 March 2009. Here is Clydevista Hyperschool, extensively modernised, 'floodwired', generously equipped with ICT resources and access to the Web in every room. History has fared better than most departments. It is equipped with 15 state-of-the-art colour portables in each room, a provision frequently supplemented by pupils who carry their own systems. Each room has colour printers, digital scanners and cameras, mobile phones for use on fieldwork (for direct on-line transfer of photographs and video), large screen displays and video-conferencing facilities. In Room 21 the pupils of class IA, who have lived and breathed high technology from birth, move purposefully between the facilities investigating History topics or solving History-oriented questions and issues. Mr. Groves has at last realised the potential of ICT in History!

Pupils access the New Education Web for Scotland (NEWS) constantly. They all have personal, specially assigned 'intelligent agents' which constantly trawl NEWS and bring to their master's attention relevant facts, pictures and significant sites which might help them in their studies. Pupils (like JimBlair@ClydeHS.ac.uk) regularly e-mail other pupils, libraries, university staff and amateur and professional historians all over the world, video-conferencing as and when necessary. They 'lurk' in chat rooms and contribute to History discussion groups. They use sophisticated multimedia tools to create impressive presentations which they store on Digital Video Disc (DVD) or submit to the Departmental website or other appropriate websites around the world. Pupils in this school are prolific contributors to global knowledge!

Fact or Fiction?

Of the above scenarios the first two are both accurate and truthful – the third, while future gazing is always a dangerous exercise, is eminently feasible and probably an understatement. ICT has developed so quickly that education has been caught on the hop. Major advances in the power and capability of the hardware and in the sophistication and the applications of the software have been matched by a growing awareness of the educational uses of ICT. However, integrating these applications into the curriculum experiences of pupils has been difficult to effect.

Phenomena like word processing, databases and spreadsheets burst like tsunami on education. Before a strategy could be formulated to exploit each of them technology was spawning newer and more powerful applications – multimedia, hypermedia and the Internet. This will continue, hopefully more slowly – refreshing and expanding ICT's potential for enhancing learning and teaching in History, for fostering enquiry and research in History and for promoting understanding and conceptual development in History.

From the early 1980s historians have been well aware that the microcomputer presented opportunities and challenges for both teacher and pupil in the History classroom.[5] Perhaps the past 20 years reflects a period of experimentation where ICT has not always been used wisely or effectively. Some critics point to 'where ICT is being poorly used it is replicating some of our worst classroom practice on a grand scale'.[6] Others criticise the lack of tangible returns from the not inconsiderable investment.[7]

In the past, currently, and increasingly in the future, the key issue is whether History teachers can harness and exploit this expanding potential of ICT. The best and most effective features and applications of ICT must be taken and built into the curriculum experiences of all pupils, giving them breadth and progression of experience.

Justifying the Role of ICT in History Teaching

It is ironic that History, with such a rich information and resource base – the data and detail of so many civilisations, accounts of battles and wars, census information on thousands of communities at many points in time, biographical and autobiographical detail, transcripts of events, video evidence, music, maps and plans, library and museum resources, artefacts and historic sites – can only offer a trivial sliver of this to pupils during their entire school career.

The major advances which have been made in ICT, notably the digitisation of information and the dimension of communication, should ensure that much more of this vast, multi-faceted treasure trove of information is accessible to all pupils.

It is important to stress that ICT does not just offer the means of making this digitised information resource accessible – it also offers a range of extremely powerful, sophisticated conceptual tools which can help access, locate, retrieve, process, analyse and repackage the information, identifying meaningful relationships and patterns and assisting the development of conclusions.

ICT could and should enhance learning and teaching in all areas of History. The argument for increasingly exploiting ICT in History teaching is not based simply on providing access to data but rather in ensuring pupils have opportunities to use and refine these information retrieval, processing and presentation skills.

Information at Their Fingertips or Information Overload?

There are many different software applications which can be deployed to great advantage in the History classroom. These can be interwoven to provide an integrated set of experiences which can foster, and capitalise on, pupil ICT skills.

Word Processing, Text Handling, Desk Top Publishing (DTP)

These can be used with all levels of pupils and offer a range of activities from the simple sequencing of text to supporting extended and creative writing.[8] Pupils can be set the task of writing simple articles to explore propaganda or bias, outlining different interpretations of events in History, or creating factual reports on topics or issues. These can be embellished with graphics. Newspaper format software and most integrated word processing packages allow teachers to create templates into which pupils can type appropriate content resulting in a *Frontline Daily* or *Jacobite Journal*.

The problems associated with developing word processing in History include the lack of systems available in the classroom and the relatively limited word processing skills of many pupils. Teachers often feel they just cannot afford the time for all pupils to create some reports. However, more equipment is arriving and pupil skills are improving. Many pupils have computers of their own at home. It is important to spread these word processing tasks out over the year, rather than involve all pupils in creating documents at the same time.

Another advantage of the more powerful and integrated packages is that they incorporate opportunities to include graphics and create, with relative ease, high quality DTP materials.

Concept Keyboards

These are seldom used in secondary schools as they are often viewed as being for the very young and the less able. This is disappointing as pupils find them an excellent way to interact with the computer and the resource can be used to great advantage in 'personalising' work – tailoring the graphical resources or text on the overlay to particular pupil ability.

Different sections of graphical overlays (a castle, a battle map or an historical environment) on top of the touch sensitive keyboard can be programmed to produce appropriate screen text responses, for example, when the illustrated section of the castle kitchen is touched the screen text might describe the kitchen, the cooking utensils and ingredients and could also list the kitchen staff and their jobs. Alternatively a selection of text could be presented on different parts of the overlay and, by simply pressing the different words or phrases, the pupil could then create a tightly focused report. Concept software effectively allowed teachers to produce Hypertext or Hypermedia resources before Hypertext software came along!

Early in their development they were used to help children identify the different parts of castles and for a simulated archaeological dig where different overlays represented five levels of the Saqarra Pyramid complex in Egypt. The beauty of this software is that targeted resources for any History topic can be developed.

Simulations and Role Play

These are the educationally acceptable 'games' representations of real life scenarios, modeled from detailed evidence of an event, battle, journey or expedition and are often very realistic and complex. Early computer simulations were simplistic, even trivial, and followed a pattern of offering selected information on which a decision had to be made. Depending on the decision the computer followed an appropriate line of action and presented fresh information. Using *Into the Unknown* pupils could 'discover' Africa and exploit its resources if they managed to sail in the right direction and correctly answer the questions.[9] Alternatively they could choose to re-enact the *Attack on the Somme*.[10] Most early simulations were time consuming, frequently reinforced pupil misconceptions, did not develop real problem solving and seldom enhanced the learning experience.

Some were excellent and have survived. *The Oregon Trail* changed as computer systems became increasingly sophisticated and exploits to the full the new facilities.[11] Pupil groups, financed by random sums of money with which they purchase food, equipment, medical supplies and oxen; travel in covered wagons from Oregon to California experiencing the vicissitudes of the early settlers. The groups have to plan their route and how fast they should travel, how they should ration their food and cross rivers, react to potentially hostile forces, cope with disease and disasters and budget finances. They can speak to fellow travellers, employ guides and buy or barter resources at various forts and settlements along the way.

In its early form this simulation was purely text-based, then it incorporated limited graphics, today the CD-ROM makes great use of multimedia facilities and groups of pupils can even travel the trail with other groups from different schools or countries on the Internet-based version. Interaction is greatly enhanced – colourful characters can be interrogated, detailed information accessed, and screen displays dynamically illustrate the progress of the intrepid settlers as they cross the North American environment.

Such improvements in technology and increased sophistication of the software are important to help enhance the learning and teaching process and to establish understanding more effectively. Equally critical is the way any simulation is used by the teacher. Even the most motivating simulation will not ensure pupils acquire the desired content and understand the processes/concepts. The teacher has to brief the pupils before running the simulation and debrief them effectively afterwards. One of the most valuable elements of *The Oregon Trail* is the 'log' of decisions which records the decisions the pupil groups make. This can be printed out at any time so that the teacher, and indeed other groups, can assess and question these decisions. This process of justifying decisions helps demonstrate understanding of circumstances and of factors operating in the environment.

Simulations can certainly help understanding, can enhance conceptual awareness, can promote decision making and stimulate critical and even creative thinking but the teacher must actively support all these facets of the learning process.

Databases and Spreadsheets

These two broad applications offer tremendous resources to the History teacher. Unfortunately to date, their potential has by no means been effectively exploited and indeed many History teachers have disdained their use. Certainly more development and interest has been accorded to databases.

In every country there are considerable collections of historical data – the census, trade and production data, weather statistics, factory workforce details, births-marriages-deaths, gravestone inscriptions – of which, so far, there has only been partial digitisation into elementary datafiles for subsequent analysis. Some pioneers have created files for school-based use – a most time consuming labour of love!

Perhaps one reason why files like these have so far met with rather limited enthusiasm in History teaching is because they only provide a microcosm of society for examination or analysis. Over the years a relatively small group of enthusiastic teachers have created databases primarily for use in their own school, for example on a village of 400 people near Airdrie in *Caldercruix 1881*, a register of dead of the *Clydebank Blitz* or the employment force affected by the *Blantyre Mining Disaster*.[12] These all contain rich data and exhibit interesting relationships if thoughtfully questioned. However, such files were often considered parochial and any observed relationships unrepresentative of national trends.

In addition, with the notable exception of packages like *Bowbridge* and the *Moving House*; *Glasgow, A Tale of Two Cities?*; *Tiree, Famine and Clearance 1840– 1900* and *Doon the Watter* series from Peter Hillis, which incorporated specially written search routines suitable for young pupils, the questioning interface was awkward and unfriendly.[13] Most pupils and many teachers had difficulty in framing a hypothesis or designing appropriate questions which would test that hypothesis. Often databases require reading and operational skills well beyond the abilities of younger pupils – who are unable to formulate and input the questions they would like answered.[14]

Recently major programmes have funded the creation of national databases and increasingly developmental projects will seek to make data from the past accessible to people of the present and the future.[15] A broad sweep of significant databases will result – often in multimedia format. The relationships which can be drawn from their analysis will be both reliable and will exemplify the national picture. In addition the databases will encompass many time periods and thus trends may be discerned.[16] Much of the data could have a mappable component (or be linked to digitised historical maps) and, in an instant, fresh relationships and distributions could be identified.[17]

Given these resources pupils could be realistically expected to set up hypotheses and then analyse data to prove or disprove them – working as real researchers (guided by their teachers). Coupled with the increasingly user friendly text and graphics software pupils could simply copy and paste the results of their investigations into a multimedia report.

Multimedia Stacks and Multimedia Authoring

The realisation of the hypertext and hypermedia ideals with software such as *HyperCard*, and more recently *HyperStudio*, opened up the possibility of creating History resources which integrated text, graphics, sound and motion.[18] Not only could general resources be developed for all pupils but, with a few conceptual leaps, a bit of imagination and a fair input of effort, materials could be designed and developed for the appropriate reading and ability level of groups or individual pupils.

In addition to pupils being the recipients of 'received information' the software also afforded pupils the opportunity to create their own multimedia presentations, fitting the multimedia pieces together like Lego bricks. Pupils could be engaged in the development of many skills – researching, collecting, organising and linking information, considering the appropriateness of different media resources and considering how best to present information to appropriate audiences. In a History classroom such multimedia reporting is particularly valuable in terms of project or topic work and local area investigation.

Software which facilitates the creation of a timeline is one multimedia resource which can double as teacher presentation tool or provide opportunities for pupil authoring. A simple timeline showing events and associated dates may be of minimal value – integrate and embellish this with resources drawn from various mediums, harness the presentational possibilities of hypermedia and you have a complex resource which can be dipped into at various points to give expanded detail. A Battle of Britain timeline could comprise textual detail on key events, pictures of aircraft or war aces, video of a dogfight and eyewitness descriptions.

Chronicle, innovative timeline software developed by the Scottish Council for Educational Technology (SCET), allows the user, either teacher or pupils, to create a timeline with the key events marked and then add to each event, if wished, textual explanation, a graphic, a video clip, and even a sub-timeline.[19] On any sub-timeline all of the aforementioned features can be added. Users only have to identify the content, detail and resources they wish to include – the software takes care of the presentation of the material.

CD-ROM

The development of this resource exemplifies the rapid rise in electronic information storage capacity which characterised the 1990s. Disc capacity suddenly jumped from 100k on floppies to 650 megabytes on CD-ROMs! As all the diverse types of information could be digitised and the hypermedia tools became available to software developers, huge collections of data were put onto CD-ROM. Today there are well over 200 History CD-ROMs, or CD-ROMs with some History content, on the market. These cover diverse topics like *World War* I, *Ancient Lands, Exploring Castles, Scottish Wars of Independence, Doon the Watter, World of the Vikings, Women's Rights,* the *Photobase*

Decades series and *Industrial Revolution* as well as complete encyclopaedias like *Grolier* and *Encarta*.[20]

There is evidence that technologies like CD-ROM that include a variety of media help pupils form rich representations of an event and cultivate deeper and more rounded understanding.[21] Pupils may be encouraged to think more creatively and critically. In addition, in a specifically historical context, where CD-ROMs present both pictorial and textual renderings from several perspectives they can help dissolve single-dimensional perspectives and can counter bias and all the stereotypical ways of thinking that impede deeper understanding. There is also a school of thought that maintains an experience that encourages understanding in a closed environment like a CD-ROM may ultimately benefit pupils more than unlimited access to unstructured information on the Internet.

However, as with any facet of ICT, the teacher should not simply expose pupils to this rich information and media mix and assume that they will learn.[22] CD-ROM use in the classroom needs to be carefully planned, the critical aspects on the disc which will contribute to learning isolated and pupils directed to specific tasks. While using CD-ROMs pupils often appear engaged and highly motivated but they may actually understand and learn very little. Much of the content is inappropriate with regard to reading level, complexity of argument and detail. Often it is not relevant to the curriculum/syllabus followed in the school.

CD-ROMs present teachers with challenging resources and it is important that teachers vet or review these resources very carefully before they even try to integrate them into their classroom activity. Word of mouth recommendation is valuable as is trialling at a local centre or at SCET's drop-in facility. Failing these one of the best sources of information on the educational value of these resources is to be found on the Virtual Teachers Centre of the National Grid for Learning.[23]

The Internet and World Wide Web (WWW)

This is the 'killer' application on which so many educational hopes are pinned. Certainly, if it can be accessed, there is an enormous educational resource to be tapped. If this resource is searched rather than surfed it can provide rich resources to complement and enhance classroom provision. The Web contains information on every subject imaginable and certainly on every aspect and time period of History. While some content is of an undesirable nature there is a surfeit of excellent material which can make a massive contribution to learning and teaching.

Once again pupils will need guidance to isolate relevant information. Teachers need to know not only the key sites to visit – including jumping off sites where useful History addresses are kept together – but also how to help pupils search for information and suggest the most appropriate search engines to use.[24] There are many skills associated with formulating a search – particularly one which will focus on a narrow segment of information and will reduce time spent at the keyboard.

There are literally hundreds of search engines, like *Excite*, *Lycos* and *Infoseek*, each with their own characteristics, and their own disciples.[25] Mastering the intricacies of their respective Power, Advanced or Phrase Searches is a necessary part of the 'fun' of using the Web. Many users turn to Meta Search Engines which effectively send out a number of search engines at the same time and then collect all the findings. A favourite is *Mamma Mia* but *Web Crawler* and *Northern Light* are also recommended as they really do save time – lots of time![26]

There are a number of History-oriented sites which have become firmly established and are highly rated. Use of these sites provides pupils with a rich set of resources – the task for the teacher is to force the pupils to view the sources critically and to discriminate and select appropriate information.

On the National Grid for Learning site there is a developing list of appropriate History sites evaluated by teachers and, at the Scottish Virtual Teachers Centre under the banner of Curriculum Resources, there are sites for 5–14 Environmental Studies (including Inside the Pyramids and Hyper History), for Standard Grade History (including the Public Record Office, America 1900, Museum of Scotland, and World War One Archive) and for Higher Still (Scots at War, America 1900 and the History Channel-Classroom).[27]

E-mail and Conferencing

While it is possible to use the Internet for e-mail there are other communications facilities in many schools, notably the First Class system. This is extremely easy to use and was used to great advantage in a national Superhighways project organised by staff on both the Aberdeen and Dundee campuses of Northern College. Many educational uses of e-mail are simply nineties versions of pen-pal letters but the Superhighways Teams Across Rural Schools (STARS) project was very different.[28]

Teachers in small rural schools were asked to identify one or two able pupils who then collaborated electronically with pupils in other, distant rural schools to consider and solve problems (on a science-based Star Trek theme but equally it could have had a History dimension) which a team in Northern College had devised. This team monitored the project, constantly sending advice and encouragement to the groups and developing new, and very different, problems for the pupils. This project, highly praised in the

Superhighways evaluation report, certainly pointed up the value of collaboration and illustrated the potential of ICT for stimulating critical and creative thinking.[29]

The model could equally be applied to a History topic. All it requires is original thought and organisation to foster collaboration between Primary and Secondary schools or between interested Secondary schools.

Video-Conferencing

A logical extension of the e-mail and WWW interaction is the use of video-conferencing. Some schools have expensive video-conferencing equipment, used very effectively in schools in Argyll and Bute and in some West Lothian Language Departments to link to pupils in foreign schools.

There are also cheap but effective 'golf-ball cameras' and software which allows pupils to video-conference with other schools who have similar equipment. The resultant video-conference is slightly jerky, but is in colour and accompanied by high quality sound and only costs the price of a local telephone call!

As the quality of the transmitted picture improves this could prove a very valuable ICT resource with great potential for visiting distant environments and discussing historical issues.

Here's Tae Us – Wha's Like Us?

Despite the alleged versatility of ICT and the proven value of many of the applications referred to above History is far from being a front-runner in the ICT-use Scottish education stakes. While many History teachers use ICT effectively and imaginatively in their classrooms and significant educational resources have been developed in Scotland for use in learning and teaching in History, ICT has failed to gain universal acceptance and support.

A number of factors have inhibited the use of ICT. For many years the lack of hardware and the inability of that hardware to cope with the information storage demands of historians and present the material in an interesting or motivating way tended to discourage all but the enthusiastic ICT-committed teacher of History. Even deploying groupwork strategies and a stations approach to learning it was difficult to make much use of ICT with only one computer in the classroom. That computer was often a humble model compared to the sophisticated machines in Business Studies or Computing Studies classrooms.

The software which seemed so advanced at the time was, in retrospect, pretty trivial and too often delivered either ridiculously simplistic or biased material. In the case of datahandling resources the software interface was too complex for children to use or the data too limited to return meaningful conclusions. Teachers frequently were disappointed to find that time invested in using the technology derived little or no significant educational return. It was often easier, and more educationally desirable, to use tried and tested non-ICT resources.

However, the ICT scene has changed dramatically. The choice of computer is simple – a Windows PC or a Macintosh. Both offer huge memory (from one to five gigabytes is now normal), run software extremely quickly, offer a built-in CD-ROM and are easily linked to the Internet/WWW. Peripheral devices like printers and scanners, even digital cameras, are of high quality and resolution but are extremely cheap and easy to use in comparison to their predecessors. Commercial software is more sophisticated and there is a wider choice of resources, although much of the software is still not specifically relevant to the Scottish History curriculum demands.

Curricular guidance and support has been very different in Scotland compared to south of the border. In Scotland Computing Studies and Business Studies departments have been relied upon to deliver desirable pupil ICT skills. While advice on IT was part of 5-14 Environmental Studies and IT was identified as a 'core skill' in Higher Still there was little genuine effort to stimulate cross-curricular ICT and ICT inclusion or permeation is a vaguely expressed hope rather than a requirement.[30] Naturally this inhibited the impact and uptake of ICT in many subjects and moves to stimulate ICT use in History came more from the interested grassroots of the profession – teachers, advisers and the Scottish Association of Teachers of History (SATH) – rather than curriculum development bodies.

In England and Wales the development of ICT in History was very deliberately fostered and this is reflected in a greater uptake of ICT in History teaching. The National Curriculum Guidelines required that History pupils 'should be given opportunities, where appropriate, to develop and apply their IT capability in their study of History' and curriculum bodies and professional organisations worked together to produce papers and support resources.[31]

Bodies like the SOEID, the Scottish Consultative Council on the Curriculum (SCCC) and SCET have recently, however, in their different ways – through ICT competence identification, Website development, CD-ROM production – tried to stimulate ICT development in History and have supported or created some excellent resources for use in schools.[32] Software development which has teacher involvement in its creation to ensure the resources are curriculum friendly and relevant, as well as being at the right level for the pupils, is still desperately needed.

The New Opportunities Fund in-service training which will be delivered from May 1999 onwards will help boost interest in ICT in History. This training is designed to be pedagogical rather than technical and will help teachers to consider the educational potential of the resource and to develop strategies for use of ICT in their classrooms. At the same time as the training is delivered schools will be supported in re-equipping and in expanding equipment provision with advanced computers (new or refurbished) which can be used to exploit the potential of the new and powerful applications mentioned earlier, particularly the Internet.

Schools will be encouraged to link to the Internet/WWW to contribute to the achievement of the current government's philosophy of a connected society. Once on the Web they will have access to the National Grid for Learning resources and, in particular, to the Virtual Teachers Centre and the Scottish Virtual Teachers Centre where advice on using ICT, reviews of CD-ROMs and Internet sites, and a comprehensive selection of resources can be accessed. In all areas a History focus will be maintained.

A Brave New World in a Brave New Millennium

Many people have a dream for the millennium. In respect of ICT in History teaching in Scottish schools the author's dream is one where all the staff have either used ICT at university and been shown how to deploy it effectively during their teacher training or have successfully undertaken the Lottery funded training. In addition they can turn, at any time, to specialised History Teaching resources on the Web which will take them patiently and encouragingly through new software and classroom management techniques or update them on resources which they can download for classroom use. As a result they have been persuaded that ICT has much to offer learning and teaching. They are critical converts!

They teach in rooms which are well equipped with robust, state of the art computers (hopefully state of the art computers will become robust) with at least one computer to every two pupils. All computers have CD-ROM or DVD drives built-in, there are scanners, digital cameras and colour printers a-plenty and a facility for large-screen display (valuable for stimulating discussion or illustrating graphics, animations or videos). Ideally the teachers are not fazed by pupils bringing their personal computers into class and are happy to bring in their own portable – supplied as an essential tool by the education authority. All of the systems offer unfettered access to the Internet – sensitive software filtering out undesirable sites – and all staff and pupils have assigned intelligent agents which crawl about the Internet and deliver information about the most relevant sites which should be visited, having been matched to individual educational interests and tasks. There are also video-conferencing resources.

Most of the resources pupils turn to are on the Web – where there is a comprehensive (and comprehensible) National Grid for Learning with sections for teachers and a vast selection of History sites which support the curriculum (freely copiable text, graphics and movies). This resource base is supported by a national ICT body (a merged SCET and SCCC) which generates new curriculum specific software and courseware for schools in all subject areas.

Importantly this is not a dream world where everything is done using ICT. Skilled History teachers only use the ICT resource when it is relevant and is the most effective way of teaching a particular aspect of History or establishing a particular concept. While ICT offers access to rich educational environments and resources its use does not necessarily or automatically mean that learning and teaching is advanced. The power of ICT has been harnessed, carefully considered and directed to result in significant improvements in learning and teaching.

The staff recognise that different pupils have different sets of intelligences and respond in different ways to different content, media and presentation. They have used the ICT toolset to develop differentiated materials and to present these materials in different ways. The History teachers constantly monitor and assess how their pupils learn and provide custom made learning materials and educational opportunities for them to explore. The acquisition of technology skills is simply viewed as a means to an end and pupils are encouraged to use a variety of appropriate ICT applications in a wide range of different classroom contexts.

Dream world perhaps but, like Clydevista Hyperschool, eminently feasible, certainly realisable and hopefully understated!

Notes

1. A Census Database project co-ordinated by Jim McArthur and Alison Gray of Strathclyde Region which produced 1851/1881 datafiles and supportive teaching resources for nine locations in West Central Scotland. Strathclyde Regional Council. 1986–1989.

2. Peter Wakefield, *Using Graveyards and Cemeteries for Investigations*. Northern College-Dundee, 1993.

3. Fernleaf Software, *Viking England*, London, 1984.
   Newman College, *Front Page Extra*, Birmingham, 1984.
   Tressell Publications, *Wagons West*, Brighton, 1986.

4. Software Toolworks, *Grolier Multimedia Encyclopaedia 97*, California, 1997.
   Peter Hillis, *Tiree, Famine and Clearance 1840–1900*, University of Strathclyde, 1996.
   Dorling Kindersley, *Eyewitness History of the World*, London, 1998.
   Past Forward, *World of the Vikings*, York, 1994.
   News Multimedia Ltd., *World War Two*, Leighton Buzzard, 1996.

5. Jim McArthur. 'The Microcomputer in the History Classroom: Opportunities and Challenges for Pupils and Teachers'. In *Historians, Computers and Data:Applications in Research and Teaching*. Editors: Mawdsley, Morgan, Richmond and Trainor. Manchester, 1990. pp 99–104.

6. Christine Counsell, 'Editorial', *Teaching History*, Issue 93, November 1998. p 2.

7. Todd Oppenheimer, 'The Computer Delusion', *The Atlantic Monthly*, Vol. 280, No. 1, July 1997. p. 45–62.

   Also at http://www.TheAtlantic.com/issues/97jul/computer.htm

8. A valuable website (part of the Virtual Teachers' Centre) offering a series of ideas on using word processing in different historical contexts is: http://vtc.nfgl.gov.uk/resources/cits/History/usingwp.html

9. Tressell Publications, *Into the Unknown*, Brighton, 1982.

10. Tressell Publications, *Attack on the Somme*, Brighton, 1984.

11. Minnesota Educational Computing Consortium (MECC), *The Oregon Trail*, Minnesota, 1991.

    Iona Software, *Oregon Trail II*, (CD-ROM), Dublin, 1994.

12. Derek Dryden, *Caldercruix 1881*, 1988.

    Robert Munro, *The Clydebank Blitz*, 1988.

    Authors unknown, *Blantyre Mining Disaster*, 1986.

13. Scottish Council for Educational Technology (SCET), *Bowbridge Pack* (A database on factory accidents in a Dundee jute factory in the nineteenth century), Glasgow, 1992.

    Peter Hillis, *Moving House*, A Resource Pack and database for Teachers and Students Analysing the Development of Certain Commercial and Residential Areas of Glasgow, 1830–1920, University of Strathclyde, 1992.

    Peter Hillis, *Glasgow, A Tale of Two Cities?*, University of Strathclyde, 1994.

    Peter Hillis, *Tiree, Famine and Clearance 1840–1900*, University of Strathclyde, 1996.

    Peter Hillis, *Doon the Watter*, University of Strathclyde, 1998.

14. Kerry Feedman and Greg Sales. 'Children's Use of Narrative and Graphical Information in a Database: Recommendations for Development'. *Journal of Research on Computing in Education*, Vol. 30, No. 4, 1998. p. 329–340.

15. Information on resources/projects developed by the Scottish Cultural Resources Access Network (SCRAN) can be accessed at: http://www.scran.ac.uk/projects

16. For example the section of The National Archives of Ireland website dealing with Transportation Records for 1791–1868 can be accessed at: http://www.nationalarchives.ie/search01.html

17. Lez Smart. 'Maps, ICT and History: A Revolution in Learning', *Teaching History*, Issue 93, November 1998. p. 28–31.

18. Apple Computer Inc. *HyperCard*, California, 1990.

    Robert Wagner Publishing, *HyperStudio*, California, 1997.

19. SCET, *Chronicle*, Glasgow, 1997.

20. News Multimedia, *World War One*, Leighton Buzzard, 1996.

    Microsoft Corporation, *Ancient Lands*, 1994.

    Anglia Multimedia, *Exploring Castles*, Norwich, 1997.

    Dunedin Multimedia, *Virtual Castle/Scottish Wars of Independence*, Edinburgh, 1998.

    Peter Hillis, *Doon The Watter*.

    Past Forward, *World of the Vikings*.

    News Multimedia, *Women's Rights*, Leighton Buzzard, 1996.

    Hulton Deutsch, *Photobase Decades*, London, 1993.

    Anglia Multimedia, *Industrial Revolution*, Norwich, 1997.

    Software Toolbooks, *Grolier Multi-media Encyclopaedia*, 97.

    Microsoft Corporation, *Encarta 95*, 1995.

21. Shirley Veenema and Howard Gardner. 'Multimedia and Multiple Intelligences', *The American Prospect*. No. 29, Nov–Dec 1996. p. 69–75. Also at: http://epn.org/prospect/29/29veen.html

22. Terry Hayden, 'Thinking, Computers, and History', *History Computer Review*. Vol. 12, 1996. p.13–23.

23. A set of History CD-ROM reviews can be found at: http://vtc.ngfl.gov.uk/vtc/class/reviews.html

24. Typical 'jump-off' sites include: http://History.cc.ukans.edu/History/WWW/History_main.html http://www.theHistorynet.com/

25. *Excite* is at: http://www.excite.com/ *Lycos* is at: http://www.lycos.com/ *Infoseek* is at: http://infoseek.go.com/

26. *Mamma Mia* is at: http://www.mamma.com/ *Web Crawler* is at: http://www.webcrawler.com/ *Northern Light* is at: http://www.northernlight.com/

27. The evaluated History websites can be accessed at: http://vtc.ngfl.gov.uk/resource/cits/History/review.html The Scottish Virtual Teachers' Centre is at: http://www.svtc.org.uk

28. Joanna McPake, John Hall, Bridget Somekh. 'Using ICT in the Primary Classroom', *Scottish Council for Educational Research (SCRE) Spotlight No. 70*. Edinburgh, 1999. Also at: http://www.scre.ac.uk/spotlight/spotlight70.html

29. Peter Scrimshaw, *Preparing for the Information Age: Synoptic Report of the Education Departments' Superhighways Initiative*, Department for Education and Employment et al., 1998.

30. Scottish Office Education and Industry Department (SOEID), *Environmental Studies 5–14*, Edinburgh, 1993.

   Scottish Consultative Council on the Curriculum (SCCC), *Higher Still: Core Skills*. Edinburgh, 1995.

31. National Council for Educational Technology (NCET) and the Historical Association worked together to produce 'History using IT – A Pupil's Entitlement'.

32. For example a CD-ROM distributed to all Scottish Secondary schools: SCCC, *The Scottish People 1840–1940. A Social and Economic History*, Edinburgh, 1998.

10

Active Teaching Methodologies

Sandra Chalmers

Introduction

It is a well known fact that pupils retain a greater percentage of knowledge when they are actively involved in gaining it, rather than acting as receptors for aural or visual information. This has led to the proliferation of projects and investigations in many subjects and has reached the extent that many pupils groan at the thought of yet another project.

This Chapter is concerned with involving pupils in other activities where they can use the historical knowledge already gained to empathise with the lives of those they have been studying. Such activity can lead to a greater depth of understanding of the period and the lives and problems of the people being studied.

The advent of the computer has led to simulations, role play and decision making scenarios which enhance learning and teaching .The problem is often that these are only of peripheral value to the courses being taught. The pupils do benefit from interacting with the program and many are written to allow group work so pupils also interact with each other.

Given the problems of finding time and tempering imagination with practical application the best activity is to involve the pupils in making games which relate to the work they are doing.

Reasons for the Approach

I was brought up in a family where we played board and card games together. Then, as an undergraduate I participated in week long reading parties at the Burn near Edzell. Without cars to take us out of the grounds, we had to make our own entertainment in the late evenings. Since the themes of the week were to do with our studies in medieval History I devised a twelfth-CENTURY medieval monopoly with cathedrals instead of stations, the arch-bishoprics of Canterbury and York instead of Mayfair and Park Lane. The cards lifted in the course of the game admonished people to go on crusade or to hide their wives and daughters since the king was due on a visit. Thirty years later, I have fond memories of staff and students playing the game into the early hours of the morning.

As a young teacher, I was faced with a class of 25 fourth year, non-certificate pupils and the problems of devising a course for them. They had considerable learning difficulties, little or no motivation and displayed considerable behavioural problems – particularly for the double period on Friday afternoon. I was at my wits' end until I remembered the pleasure of making up medieval monopoly.

I re-thought my strategy and set weekly work targets which were displayed in the classroom. If pupils could meet those targets in the four 40-minute periods earlier in the week, they could devote the double period on Friday afternoon to devise games related to their work on the mining industry in the nineteenth century. Once those games were completed they were allowed to play them. Within a month, the work rate had increased, the in-discipline had declined and fewer pupils were playing truant. At the time, my motives were pragmatic. I was only too glad that my life was easier but , in retrospect, I was able to analyse why the idea had been a success and judge that it had considerable educational value:

(a) the novelty of the approach was obviously one factor in success, as it opened up a new learning experience which brought greater variety to my teaching;

(b) it provided pupils with motivation to complete the normal work of the class so they could tackle something new and more interesting;

(c) participation in devising a game in a format of their choice gave pupils a sense of ownership of the finished product. They enjoyed the social interaction of working in groups and an element of competition appeared as they sought to produce a game which they perceived as superior to the games of other groups in the class;

(d) the stages involved in making the game helped them by reinforcing their knowledge of the historical facts and leading to greater empathy with the people involved in mining in the nineteenth century;

(e) since each member of the group wanted to contribute something, it gave individuals a chance to use particular skills, however limited, such as drawing straight lines, drawing or colouring in illustrations, making cards for penalties and bonuses;

(f) in completing the work the groups were actually using social, practical, intellectual and problem solving skills.

These lessons are ones I have not forgotten in my subsequent teaching career. Where appropriate, and where I have had time, I have expanded the variety of games for use in teaching.

Examples of Games

Board Games

These are perhaps the simplest type of games to devise and can be enjoyed by pupils of all ages and abilities. The pupils can tailor the format to any game with which they are familiar.

Medieval Monopoly

This game was set in twelfth-century Angevin England and the properties included ports, towns, monasteries, royal hunting lodges, the arch-bishoprics. Chance and Community Chest were replaced with Chancery and Exchequer cards. Players represented by plastic knights paid fines at bridge tolls, demesne mills or for disturbing the king's peace. They went on crusade instead of going to jail. Instead of increasing property and fines for building houses, the value increased as the property held 1–4 knights. Modern monopoly's hotel was transformed into a castle.

Money could be won for being made an earl, winning tournaments, selling your ward in marriage; while losses were incurred for such things as ransoming the body of your lord, falling foul of the ecclesiastical courts or causing a damsel to be in distress.

A similar game might be based on the growth of the medieval burgh or a medieval castle.

Mining Games

In these games devised by the non-certificate class of my youth, the pupils used their knowledge of the three main stages of a mining operation: hewing the coal from the coal face, moving the coal underground and raising the coal to the surface. Pupils divided the board into these three sections. One successful board used the snakes and ladders format, with the winner being the first to bring the coal to the surface; another borrowed from ludo and had colliers bringing four loads of coal to the surface while a third had four mines, each taking up one side of the board. A fourth, enterprising group had a spiral route from the centre to one outside corner of the board. The areas not used for squares were decorated with drawings of mining equipment and members of the mining family.

They devised penalties and bonuses connected with the stages above and placed them on appropriate squares of the board. Penalties were involved with dangers such as gas, cave-ins, poor ventilation and floods and the penalties varied from going back a number of squares, missing turns and being killed and having to start from the beginning. Bonuses often arose from mining improvements such as the safety lamp, using pit props instead of pillars of coal, changing bearers to putters, raising coal with a steam engine instead of a horse-drawn gin. The rewards involved such things as moving forward or gaining extra throws of the dice.

The Suffragettes

Our pupils have been fortunate enough to be born into a society where they have many 'rights' and they find it difficult to appreciate the difficulties and frustrations experienced by the women who fought for the vote. Often the attitude of classes seems to follow gender lines with girls empathising with the suffragettes but some boys finding them 'silly' or applauding the resort to militant tactics because of their violence and confrontations with the police.

As an extension to the topic, I have encouraged pupils to make posters or a wall frieze but I have found a Suffragette Monopoly an enhancement which enables pupils to experience a little of the frustration felt by the women and to reinforce the idea of cause and consequence by suffering punishments for breaking the law.

The objective of the game is to win a certain number of votes from M.P.s and the target set can either be a specified number of votes, for example, fifty; or the winner is the person who has gained most votes at the end of the period.

The board represents the city of London and the places identified are those which have some significance in the Suffragette campaign. The players begin at WSPU headquarters but, naturally, the Houses of Parliament and Holloway prison play important roles as the game progresses.

The players proceed round the board according to the throw of a dice. If they land on an Activity Square they have to take the top card from the centre of the board. The card identifies one of the methods used by the women and the likely result of the action: for example, a petition with 100,000 signatures might win 5 votes; presenting it to the P.M. would take the player to Downing Street; heckling meetings or chaining themselves to railings would get them arrested; being released from prison after a hunger strike would give an extra throw. If the action results in the person being arrested, the player lifts a card from the Verdict cards. Being found guilty might result in being fined one vote or going to prison and missing one or two throws

On completion of each circuit of the board , the player receives five votes. The receipt and deduction of votes for each player are recorded on a separate sheet. The deductions are particularly resented by players but are very valuable in showing that the escalation of violence lost the Suffragettes supporters as well as winning them attention.

It is not an easy game to win. By the time the unsympathetic boys in the class have lost as many votes as they have won and wasted varying amounts of time in Holloway they tend to experience some empathy for the women.

Games at Standard Grade

Margot McDonald, Depute Head Teacher at Ballerup High School, East Kilbride has used the board games idea to enhance the work of a Standard Grade section and make revision more interesting. She set aside time so that groups of pupils could take a topic from Unit 1, Changing Life in Scotland and Britain, and turn it into a game. They selected or drew two pictures which illustrated the topic. They then devised a series of cards which tested pupils' knowledge . Boards were drawn up in appropriate patterns making use of the illustrations, for example, a game on agricultural changes had one set of cards which tested knowledge on the Highlands for moving through the top half of the board, while a different set of cards tested lowland farming in the bottom half.

When the games were being played and pupils landed on certain squares, another player would pick up the card and ask the question. If it was answered correctly, the player moved on; if it was incorrect they missed a turn. In this situation pupils tended to ask searching questions of their peers, often more demanding than those the teacher might have used. Having a variety of games covering different topics, meant groups could swap games and thereby enjoy revision of much of Unit 1.

Decision Making /Role Play Games

The use of role-play to allow pupils to empathise with people in the past by looking at a historical situation through the eyes of an individual or group involved in it is a strategy which has been meandering in and out of classrooms for at least 30 years.[1] There has been considerable debate on what is meant by empathy and whether it can be taught. *Teaching History* in April 1989 devoted three articles to it and provide a good start to anyone wishing to familiarise themselves with the debate. Ann Low-Beer looks at using empathy to examine feelings and concludes that 'in the end empathy exercises are ways of making sense of historical evidence and coming to see that at other times, in other contexts, things were different.' She also notes that poems, personal letters and films are other weapons in the teacher's armoury.[2]

John Cairns takes the issue further by discussing different facets of empathy (as power, achievement, process and disposition).[3] He gives three characteristics of empathy as trying to get inside the minds of contemporaries to understand events; using evidence and reflection to try to 'achieve a knowledge of what someone (or some group believed, valued, felt and tried to achieve.' The third stage is to link beliefs, emotions and actions to the situations of the people being studied.[4]

For anyone wishing to devise their own exercise he goes on to indicate the factors necessary to allow pupils to think empathetically and looks at the cognitive abilities of pupils.[5]

Fortunately for busy teachers, others have shared their attempts at putting the ideas into practice. Robin Duff has produced an exercise to help pupils understand appeasement and Munich through the eyes of French, Germans, Sudeten Germans, Czechs, Chamberlain and Churchill.[6] It is an exercise which could prove beneficial to Intermediate and Higher pupils studying Appeasement and the Road to War.

The Bosnian Crisis 1908

My own venture into this type of activity occurred around 15 years ago when I looked round the faces of a fourth year class to whom I had been explaining, for the second time, the Balkan situation before the First World War. Using the analogy of rival gangs to explain the alliance system was something they could relate to but they could not understand why one crisis had resulted in negotiation, others in localised Balkan Wars and the assassination of Archduke Franz Ferdinand in a devastating world war. I wished them to have some idea of the interaction of the nations and an understanding of how the attitude and actions of the major powers could control the actions of smaller nations.

Over the week-end I pondered how I could resolve their confusion. After some 15 to 20 hours of research and fumbling over a format, I produced *Flashpoint – the Balkans.*

1. THE OBJECTIVES OF THE EXERCISE WERE:

   (a) to allow pupils to work in groups to make informed decisions based on knowledge of the countries involved in the Bosnian Crisis 1908;

   (b) each group would represent one of the nations and look at the options available to that nation in the crisis;

   (c) they would then make a decision on the best course of action for their country;

   (d) they would be allowed to interact with friends and potential foes to experience the ways in which larger countries could put pressure on smaller ones.

2. STAGES

   The exercise was played in three stages, each taking a single period of class time.

   THE PLANNING STAGE:

   (a) this involved dividing pupils into groups representing Austria, Serbia, Germany, Russia and Turkey. Each group had to choose a leader and a scribe;

b) each person was issued with information about themselves and the other participating nations. This gave information about head of state, type of government, population size, racial mix, religion, industrial strength, army size, allies and potential foes;

c) the class studied the information and discussed the importance of knowing such things as industrial strength and army size of friends and foes in a crisis. The opportunity was taken to recap on the alliance system and remind them how countries who shared a common enemy might find that a basis for becoming friends and allies;

d) emphasis was given to the fact that governments do not enter into war lightly because of the nature and extent of possible consequences. The alternatives were discussed (doing nothing, consulting others, using diplomatic channels, attempting to put pressure on the aggressor);

(e) I then opened pupil participation by explaining about the Austrian annexation of Bosnia and Herzegovina;

(f) each group was given a 'Crisis Management' sheet which invited them to discuss their country's situation in the crisis and to look at the various courses of action and their possible consequences. Each country had to select their course of action;

(g) the sheets were collected in at the end of the period.

3. NEGOTIATIONS:

(a) the sheets were returned to each country so they could proceed with their plans. Any group which appeared to be struggling were given a little guidance here;

(b) contact with other countries had to take place through the medium of diplomatic telegrams obtained from the teacher who numbered them as they were given to the recipients;

(c) any telegrams to France or Britain were responded to by the teacher;

(d) by looking at the content of the telegrams as they were being delivered, it was possible for the teacher to point up inconsistencies and refer countries to their information about the other players;

(e) the use of telegrams continued for the period or until a solution had been reached. In the event of war being declared the teacher declared what the outcome would have been.

4. OUTCOME/FEEDBACK:

(a) the third period was used to review the stages of interaction and the whole class were invited to comment on the suitability or otherwise of the actions of the various nations;

(b) the teacher then informed the class of the events and resolution of the actual crisis of 1908 and the actions of the class and real nations were compared.

Having undertaken this exercise for some 15 years, with classes of high ability, mixed ability, Foundation classes and classes predominantly male, female or evenly mixed, I am still surprised by the variations the exercise can provide. I have had classes whose nations' actions more or less duplicated the real crisis; I have had World War One beginning in 1908!

The vast majority of pupils respond well and do adopt the attitudes of their nation. Some have to be reminded that Cabinet Ministers have to express themselves in certain ways. However, even if Russia does send Austria a message saying 'Stop it now or we'll give you a doing!' it does indicate that empathy for the feelings of Russians has been achieved.

One of my fondest memories is of a Credit level class and a group of very able boys who were slow to respond when choosing their country and ended up as Turkey. Frustrated at the helplessness and isolation of their country, they sent Austria a telegram informing them that Turkey had been involved in secret negotiations with Britain and that Britain had been secretly building Dreadnoughts for Turkey. If Austria did not return Bosnia and Herzegovina at once they were going to have to face these Dreadnoughts. When I informed them that I could not send such a telegram because it had no basis in evidence, I was informed that bluffs were a part of diplomacy and that' all is fair in love and war – and this is war'. I asked them to look at their map of the area and pointed out that even if the Dreadnoughts had existed I didn't think Austria would be too worried about their use as they might have trouble sailing them up the Danube.

Often telegrams show a mixture of naivety and sound common sense , for example, Serbia seeking Russia's protection but offering munitions as a bribe because Russia is backward. On one occasion, Turkey sought alliances with Serbia and Russia so they could send an ultimatum to Austria. They were disappointed when Russia sent back a strong reply telling them they better finish their civil war first. During the negotiations I normally restrict myself to referring groups back to the evidence to look again at possible consequences but if they persist in an inappropriate action it is up to the other countries to act appropriately, as indeed happened when Russia squashed Turkey's attempt at seeking help.

The feedback often produces surprises over the facts which pupils have gleaned and they can be exceedingly scathing to groups who have done something out of character. A group of very aggressive boys who were representing Germany once tried to offer Russia land in the Balkans for an alliance against Austria. To my surprise, it was a timid girl who reminded them Austria had been their only friend at the Algeciras conference and they would be in big trouble if Russia showed Austria the offer. They might find themselves fighting a war on three fronts!

Despite the factual mistakes which can be made by individual pupils over the details, the role play exercise has proved a success in helping pupils understand the complexity of international diplomacy and it brings home to them that even a large country like Russia was helpless to protect her interests in 1908 and had to face the ignominy of being unable to help Serbia.

I have also found that the memory of the interaction in 1908 can carry over when classes are studying the complex train of events in the summer of 1914, for example, pupils understand why Russia mobilised when Austria bombarded Belgrade and can anticipate which country Russia will wish to consult.

A role play of this sort takes a great deal of work to set up and some classes benefit from having a co-operative teacher participating in the negotiation stage. Obviously, such a teacher has to be knowledgeable about the period so he or she can guide groups into looking at evidence and making sound judgements about the possible consequences of certain actions. All boys' groups tend to wish to represent Germany because they think it will present them with the opportunity to throw their weight about. A judicious choice of personnel in groups can make all the difference and it is valuable to have 'doves' as well as 'hawks' in Germany and Austria so aggression is tempered with common sense .

Making Your Own Games

Someone who wishes to make tentative steps into the use of games in the History class room might be wise to use an existing role play until they gain confidence but if they wish to branch out with junior classes it would be sensible to begin with devising a board game.

The following stages are offered as a pattern which can be adapted to individual needs . It is one which a class teacher can operate with a class or small group of pupils.

1. OBJECTIVE

   It is essential to establish the objective, whether it is retrieving one load of coal from the mine or obtaining support from 50 MPs for female suffrage.

2. FORMAT

   The format must be appropriate to the ability and skills of the pupils involved. If time is short or resources limited it is best to make a board which has penalties and bonuses written on specific squares. Pupils should have the opportunity to suggest layout and will often bring a board from home so they can trace the outline of squares on paper.

   More able pupils may wish to produce cards which convey instructions to players. This increases the variables in the game and can make it more exciting. It does, however require much more detailed knowledge.

3. DETAILED PLANNING

(a) In order to prepare pupils by placing them into suitable groups, individuals should be asked to indicate their strengths and development needs by placing either a G (Good at) or an I (wish to Improve) opposite the following:

using words____   seeing / drawing ____
doing things with your hands____   thinking things through____
talking to and working with people____

The teacher should then try to arrange groups to cover the skills. The rule in each group is that the people who are trying to improve should have the first opportunity at a particular task. Pupils must also have the opportunity to participate and share their strengths. At the end of the exercise pupils can be given the opportunity to provide feedback on how helpful their colleagues have been and how much they have improved.

(b) Time is saved if the right resources are available. This includes both lined and graph paper. The lined paper can be used for writing factual information and the graph paper to plan layout. Extra books for additional research and picture ideas should also be at hand.

(c) The next step is to amass the historical information needed. These should be organised according to aspects of the topic and chronology. Under the appropriate headings, lists of facts should be collected to indicate penalties (things which hinder achievement of your objective) and bonuses (things which help the achievement of your objective).

(d) When the rough draft is drawn to scale on graph paper it is sufficient to number squares where penalties and bonuses are to be placed. If cards are to be produced it is essential to look at the balance of the number of penalties and bonuses. If, as with the Suffragettes, you wish to emphasise the difficulties and frustrations of the campaign this can be achieved by including a larger proportion of penalty cards.

(e) When producing the final board, it is important to allocate tasks so everyone can make a contribution. This can take considerable diplomacy to ensure a less able or less skilled pupil does not spoil the finished product. Colouring in pictures or typing facts on a word processor can give a sense of pride to pupils.

(f) Anyone whose contribution has been very limited should be given the chance to participate in the piloting of the game as they can take pride in testing if it works. Piloting should be done on the small scale board if instructions are to be written on the board. The full size board can be used if the use of cards is involved. After the team have played the game they should watch outsiders attempt to play. If instructions or rules are inadequate they will most likely be identified by the end of this stage.

(g) The final, full size version of the game should be completed. If possible the board should be laminated to protect it. Written instructions for playing should be provided. A good game can be used by future classes and provide the department with a valuable resource.

Benefits

As departments continue the battle to raise achievement and teachers become more familiar with the latest research on how children learn, it is likely departments will try to include more active learning in their management of the curriculum. If we accept that we learn . . .

10 per cent of what we read
20 per cent of what we hear
30 per cent of what we see
50 per cent of what we both see and hear
70 per cent of what is discussed with others
80 per cent of what we experience personally
90 per cent of what we TEACH to someone else

It is likely that involving pupils in devising games and showing others how to play them is going to pay dividends in increasing achievement in knowledge and understanding.

If one accepts Howard Gardner's writings on multiple intelligences it is clear that the study of History is most involved with developing linguistic and logical/mathematical intelligence.[7] Introducing the development of games will give opportunities to develop visual/spatial intelligence (devising the board) while the group discussion and planning, the drawing up of penalties and bonuses will help improve both interpersonal and practical skills.

The different stages of the activity go beyond simple comprehension to the higher level thinking skills identified in Bloom's taxonomy. They have to apply the knowledge gained in class work and analyse and categorise the evidence. In their group discussion they evaluate the suitability of certain evidence for their purpose, they then synthesise and create their own game. The final evaluation comes after the two stage piloting when they address any problems and present their final product.

For those burdened by the implementation of the various strands of 5–14, a perusal of the strands for assessment will show that it would be possible to use the skills to assess such strands as planning and collecting, interpreting and evaluating and recording and presenting information.

In summation, it is evident that involvement in problem solving, developing games and taking part in role-plays provides not only variety to teaching methodology but it also furthers linguistic, logical, practical and cognitive skills. Most important of all, it is an experience which pupils – and even the teacher – enjoy doing. Pupils are really proud of themselves when the teacher sits down and plays a game they produced.

The Future

As we enter the third millennium pupils spend an increasing amount of time interacting with games on a computer screen. They may use their beloved computer to produce a more sophisticated historical game but through their understanding of History active learning encourages them to interact with other human beings. Their poor beleaguered History teacher has the satisfaction of knowing that a love of the subject has been passed on to pupils.

Notes

1. The Longman Group Resources Unit published a boxed set of 12 *History Games* back in 1973. These allowed pupils to take roles in such diverse situations as The Norman Conquest, Trade and Discovery, Railway Mania and the Scramble for Africa.

2. Ann Low-Beer, 'Empathy and History', *Teaching History*, No. 55, 1989 p.8–12.

3. John Cairns, 'Some Reflections on Empathy in History', *Teaching History*, No. 55, 1989, p.8–12.

4. Ibid. p.15.

5. Ibid. p.15–16.

6. Robin Duff, 'Appeasement Role Play: the Alternative to Munich', *Teaching History*, No. 90, 1998 p.17–19.

7. Howard Gardner, *Multiple Intelligences: The Theory in Practice*, (New York, 1993).

11

Using Historical Sources

E.J. Geraghty

Purposes of Using Sources in History Teaching

For many years now the use of sources in History teaching has been common. No recent textbook or study guide or research task or indeed assessment item is complete without reference to and invariably use of short source extracts whether of a written or of a visual kind. It is unlikely that such activity will decrease in the future – so why the use of sources in History teaching?

Principally sources are used in History teaching for the dramatic impact they have on lessons. There is nothing quite like the appropriate, contemporary illustration/picture or the apt, succinct and lively source extract to illustrate a point or trend or development in History. The impact of the eye-witness account of an event immediately engages pupil attention and stimulates the imagination. Detailed examination of sources by individuals or classes engages pupils' critical faculties and once engaged these can be further stimulated and extended. In other words good use of sources facilitates and makes for good teaching and learning. This is probably the principal purpose of using sources in History teaching.

A second purpose is to give pupils a taste of the real work of historians. Gradually pupils learn to treat sources not as simple statements of fact but as evidence, which, Collingwood argued, was the function of the scientific historian.[1] More modern historians, as for example Michael Lynch, describe the work of the historian in slightly fuller terms. In his *New History of Scotland* he introduces a section on the Reformation by suggesting that the purpose of the historian is not primarily didactic as it was conceived for example in an earlier age by the Scottish Reformer, John Knox. Knox thought that his account of the Reformation conveyed 'the simple truth' for all to see. The work of the modern historian, Michael Lynch argues, is more complex and seeks to present a view of the past which is not quite so simple but is sometimes 'confusing, ambiguous and often contradictory'.[2] In arriving at such an analysis or reconstruction of the past the historian considers, analyses and evaluates all the relevant evidence that comes to hand. So too in teaching – it is not the purpose of History teaching to convey received truths about the past but to engage and involve pupils in a process which attempts to reconstruct and explain the past. In pursuit of this goal, use and analysis of all kinds of sources is essential. This activity is both intellectually stimulating in its own right and extends pupils' abilities or skills considerably.

The skills involved are variously described, but involve applying knowledge and understanding of particular topics and events to the sources being studied by interpreting, analysing, synthesising, comparing sources and reaching a final evaluation. This forms part of the tradition of literary criticism of written documents to which the study of History exposes all students; a tradition of scholarship which by degrees they acquire for themselves. Such scholarship has a particular slant to it which is peculiar to the study of History. Two examples might suffice to make this point. Firstly, examining evidence from the past in the circumstances in which it was produced – putting sources into their proper historical context – is a sine qua non of such literary and historical criticism. Another equally important task is determining the possible purpose for which the sources were written or produced in the first place. As Fustel de Coulanges, a French historian of the Third Republic, put it, 'Chaqu'un n'écrit que ce qui sert'.[3] Neither of these skills is acquired without effort from the student and direction from the teacher but both make important contributions to extending pupil abilities.

Perhaps an additional purpose of using sources is to engender in pupils a degree of scepticism. As early as 1945 Karl Mannheim in *Diagnosis of Our Time* argued that one of the functions of self-education was to 'bring about a frame of mind which can bear the burden of scepticism and does not panic when many of the thought habits are doomed to vanish.'[4] It could be argued that the difficulties identified by Mannheim after the World War II have been considerably magnified today as politicians, multi-national companies and the media attempt, either deliberately or inadvertently, to impose their values upon society. The critical, partly sceptical mind, cultivated by the detailed study and analysis of sources perhaps furnishes pupils with one intellectual tool which will help them to deal with such problems. The critical study of historical sources contributes to that process.

Lastly source analysis and evaluation is one aspect of the wider contribution made by the study of History to the education of students and their preparation for life in society. In gradually learning more about people in the past – their habits, their work patterns, their achievements, their failures, their motivation etc. – students gradually learn more about themselves. The study of History engenders a respect for evidence, a mental habit of questioning evidence or received opinion, an appreciation of and acceptance of opposing points of view, a faith in democracy in all its forms and perhaps a desire to maintain democracy in the future. At the same time it passes on to future generations a sense of national identity and culture within both a European and world dimension. These processes do not happen automatically. Howard

Sharron argues in his book *Changing Children's Minds* – an examination of Feuerstein's work in Israel on the teaching of intelligence – that, 'culture is not absorbed by children, it is imposed upon them'. Acquiring a culture he describes as a 'mediated learning experience'.[5] In this connection the role of the teacher is crucial whether conveying a sense of national, cultural identity or introducing students to the traditions of historical scholarship through the critical evaluation of sources.

Typical Examples of Possible Uses of Sources in History Teaching

There is no end to the uses to which sources can be put in teaching in Secondary Schools. Pictorial or written sources are used to arouse pupil interest, to illustrate what was involved in an activity or lifestyle or event in the past. As such use of appropriate sources make the work of History classes much more interesting and enjoyable. Drawings, cartoons, paintings, photographs or written sources found in any modern textbook are useful sources of information about the past. Whole class activities or group activities either teacher directed or pupil led can easily be centered round eliciting as much information from sources as possible; similar activities obviously could be focused on limitations of sources. Simple exercises can be set in Secondary 1 and Secondary 2 classifying the sources used in a particular unit of work. Examples of such classifications might include:

Number of source	Author	Date of writing or compilation	British, Scottish or foreign origin of source	Primary or Secondary?	etc

Furthermore, sources can be used to make a straightforward reconstruction of some activity from the past from the evidence of contemporary records which brings home to pupils in a dramatic way exactly what was involved in the activity in the first place. A simple example of this might be pupil reconstructions of original interviews from the written reports of factory or mines inspectors. Class discussion or debates can be centered around the interpretation of a source or sources. Such discussions can arise naturally in the course of lessons or circumstances can be arranged leading to discussions and debates either by individuals or groups. In many schools problem solving activities, set within a particular context and centered on a specific historical problem, are regularly used. Such exercises involve pupils in problems of interpretation of evidence or reconciling conflicting evidence or exploring motivation. Often the source packs on which such activities are based are commercially produced and are excellent methods of introducing, teaching or reinforcing skills of critical evaluation of sources. Individual or class research is always source based. Such research can be informed and directed by the provision of, or search for, appropriate source materials relevant to a particular line of inquiry. Such activities can be pursued at a relatively simple level as in a typical investigation in Secondary 1 and Secondary 2 or at a much more sophisticated level as, for example, in the skills involved in researching and presenting an extended essay at Higher level or a dissertation in the Advanced Higher/Certificate of Sixth Year Studies. In each instance where research is involved critical evaluation of sources takes place. The higher up the school the more complex such research exercises become, the more sophisticated the source evaluation demanded. Critical evaluation of sources by individuals or class groups is an on-going aspect of all History classes in Secondary school. To improve pupil abilities in this area individuals can be asked to read their responses to particular evaluation questions related to material being studied. The benefits which this activity engenders are many – the individual concerned quickly realises that he/she is writing for an audience; good responses are easily identified by classmates; good examples of critical evaluation are thereby disseminated effortlessly to the whole class; poor responses elicit comments which praise relevant parts of responses and the teacher has a fairly good idea of individual and class understanding of the processes involved. This activity has its place further up the school, for example, in classes studying Higher History. The same benefits apply although some effort on the part of teachers is required to make this an acceptable activity to senior pupils. Here again class judgment of individual responses is based on agreed criteria, such as:

Clarity of response	Placing source in context	Analysis of evidence in source	Use of relevant recalled evidence in the response	Use of scholarly language	Conclusion

In many instances at this level what individual pupil responses constantly reinforce is the view that there are many different ways of producing an acceptable answer to a particular question and reaching a supported conclusion based on pupil evidence selected from sources and recalled knowledge. Picking up on such points either by the teacher or by classmates reinforces pupil confidence.

In all of these activities, and the above suggestions explore only a few possibilities, there are perhaps a few points to be made form the point of view of teaching. The first is the obvious one that evaluation of sources involves increasingly sophisticated skills the further one progresses in Secondary School. These skills cannot profitably be set aside in any year. There is need for fairly constant reinforcement. The second point to emphasise is that in these activities, whether carried out on an individual or group basis, the following stages are present:

(a) a clear task is set or devised or suggested involving the use and evaluation of sources;

(b) individuals or groups complete the task set according to fairly strict, limited criteria;

(c) individuals or groups display and present the completed tasks for teacher or whole class evaluation;

(d) identification of strengths and weaknesses of presentations is made according to fairly straightforward, agreed criteria by teacher or class.

The whole process is intended to be a confidence boosting exercise. This suggests a final point in respect of such source based activities, viz. that the skills involved are achievable and worth the achievement. In a sense teachers should aim to present such skills as achievable goals for all pupils, progressively boosting pupil confidence in their pursuit. Sharron argues in the work already referred to above that 'a child's success at solving intellectual problems is as dependent on his feelings of competence as on his actual competence – if the first is not present they (children) are so convinced of likely failure that they don't attempt to solve the problem'.[6] Experienced teachers will probably recognise the value of this observation; a useful reminder perhaps for all teachers!

Sources and Assessment in History

One of the commonest uses of sources in Scottish Schools is for assessment purposes. Here their use is dictated by the criteria on which the particular assessment or exam is focused. In Scottish schools this means 5–14 requirements in Secondary 1 and Secondary 2, Standard Grade criteria for Secondary 3 and Secondary 4 pupils and Higher and Advanced Higher/ Certificate of Sixth Year Studies requirements in the upper school. Although the skills involved at each stage are progressively more sophisticated there is sometimes an apparent mismatch of skills demanded between one level and another which should be investigated. Having said that, perhaps the following points are worth noting regarding sources used in assessments which:

(a) are selected bearing in mind the stage of development of pupils;

(b) are altered as required to make them accessible to the candidates for whom they are intended;

(c) generally contain distracters not required in responses;

(d) are generally short;

(e) are introduced by an appropriate statement re authorship, publication etc.;

(f) are not exclusively written sources.

Given these restrictions the sources sometimes seem very artificial or contrived. However by and large they are suitable for the purposes intended. Questions set on sources must:

(a) take into account stage and development of pupils;

(b) be specifically designed to test the criteria of the course followed, being based on strands in the case of 5–14; Grade Related Criteria at Standard Grade; and Outcomes and Performance Criteria in Higher Still courses;

(c) always require student judgment of the source or sources involved;

(d) invite students to use source-based evidence in responses;

(e) allow pupils to display their skills and knowledge to their best advantage;

(f) invariably demand more than source-based evidence in responses (except perhaps in some comparison questions).

Given these restrictions it could be argued that source-based History exams have served Scottish schools well. In respect of public examinations the Scottish Qualifications Authority in the past has set standards of attainment in assessments and will continue to do so. Scottish Qualifications Authority alterations to History syllabuses partly dictate what is taught in History classes and also partly how it is taught. Similarly, analysis of pupil responses to questions has led to improvements in question setting. The whole process is reviewed regularly by Scottish Qualifications Authority staff to improve questions and help avoid the dead hand of formalism descending on exams or on pupil responses. This can become a problem in source-based questions especially those involving evaluation. Formulised responses are much less common at Higher level where there is a source-handling exam paper. This may be the case for two reasons. Firstly, the source handling paper at Higher is sharply focused; there is a body of knowledge about the topic with which all pupils should be familiar and a particular section within the topic (the so-called boxed area) from which sources are taken as the basis for questions though use of information from outwith the boxed area is recognised in responses. Secondly, use of recalled knowledge is clearly expected by the questions either to set sources in context or to evaluate sources/opinions/views given. The recalled knowledge expected in such questions must of course be relevant to the question set but is not restricted in its use. A candidate can use recalled knowledge to display his abilities to his/her best advantage, the only constraint being time to complete the exam. Credit for use of relevant recalled knowledge in responses is awarded. Perhaps there is a model here for other syllabus areas where formulised responses sometimes cause concern.

Typical Examples of Pupil Responses to Source Based Questions in History in Secondary Schools

Although the sources on which the original questions were based have been omitted the pupil answers show the progression on from Secondary 1 to

Secondary 6. All of the responses below were produced in the course of assessments in John Ogilvie High School, Burnbank, a South Lanark Education Authority school. The Secondary 6 example is an extract from the conclusion to a Certificate of Sixth Year Studies dissertation from the school.

SECONDARY 1

(a) I don't think that source 32 is a completely reliable source of evidence because it was written hundreds of years after everything had happened. However I think the writers of Source 32 may have got their information from archeologists and from other people's writings like for example Bede and Gildas.

(b) The author of Source A liked William because at the start of the paragraph in Source A he says that William is very wise and great plus he's more honoured and powerful than the kings before him. The author of Source B disliked William because he says William killed many in his vengeance, burnt down houses and destroyed many people's food and belongings. The author of Source C has a balanced opinion on William because he says that he treated the poor badly and took land, gold and silver from his subjects. However he says that he built forests for deer and whoever killed a deer should be blinded. He treated the deer like sons.

SECONDARY 2

(a) The author of source 21 thinks that navvies are animals and that they are thick. He thinks they are insulting and they don't care about their past and also that they only care about themselves and no-one else.

I think source 21 is not all true. Not all navvies were like that; most of these people were like that because of the job they did. I think every person wants to learn new things; its just that they have not a lot of spare time to learn new things because they work such long hours. Also the person who wrote it might have written such nasty things about navvies just because he didn't like them.

(b) I think that of the two interpretations of city life Sources 19, 20 and 21 are more popular because they are more pleasing and more people would like to believe them. I think that the sources on pages 54–56 are more truthful because some of them are pictures which can't be altered so it is exactly as it was. As for the sources on pages 54–56, these were written very close to the time and could be very truthful in describing the conditions. The reason I say this is because I think Sources 19, 20 and 21 have been altered to make the city look nicer.

SECONDARY 3

(a) Trotsky's attitude in Source B to the events of the war and the impact of the war on troops of Russia is one of anger because he immediately identifies how many were killed – 2.5 million Russians approximately. He says this was because they were not thinking enough because of lack of experience in wars and because the lower ranks were ignorantly commanded. He is angry because officers were inexperienced and untrained and because lower ranks were badly treated.'

(b) Sources A, B and C describe conditions in Russia in World War I reasonably well. For example, Source A tells us what was happening in Riga (they would be defeated there if they didn't move fast); Source B tells us about some of the consequences of war on Russian soldiers (2.5 million killed or missing); it also tells us how tactically naive Russian officers were and Source C tells us about the conditions and equipment that the soldiers fought in or with (low ammunition and supplies). But none of the sources tell us about the effects the war was having in Petrograd or the countryside (starvation in the city, not enough peasants or horses left to work in the countryside) . The sources do not tell us anything about the living conditions that soldiers endured. They don't fully describe the conditions in Russia.

SECONDARY 4

(a) Source A is quite a useful source. It is a primary source, spoken in 1908 by an eye-witness. The author/woman is a doctor, so you would think because of her profession she wouldn't lie. Its contents include a lot about suffragettes and their militant tactics. Although Dr. Marion Gilchrist's profession means she is a respected woman she may be slightly biased as she might have been a suffragette supporter. Source B is a secondary source, although it is useful in the fact that it agrees with other sources. It is from a published book on Women in Scotland, so it is more likely to be factual. It is full of facts about tactics used by suffragettes in 1912. It states that women went to prison and went on hunger strikes.

Although the two sources talk of the Suffragette Campaign, Source A doesn't directly comment on how much good their tactics did them, although Source B does state 'They went on hunger strike . . . and aroused public sympathy'. Overall they are quite reliable and useful sources.

(b) Source C is a secondary source published in 1987 by David Stewart and James Fitzgerald. It tells us that the growth of Germany's Navy was worrying. Before 1900 German naval power had been insignificant but after that it had grown tremendously and they had built 7 battleships, 2 heavy cruisers, 7 light cruisers and other vessels. However it doesn't describe Britain's efforts to out-do Germany. In fact, it was Britain who created the H.M.S. Dreadnought, the finest battleship of World War I. The Germans copied it and by around 1914 Britain had 20 Dreadnought-class ships and Germany had 13 Dreadnought-class ships. Source C is useful in describing Germany's efforts to win the Naval Race but not the efforts of Britain.

SECONDARY 5

(a) This is a speech by the Labour opposition member in March 1936. He is talking about the German re-occupation of the Rhineland. Hugh Dalton says that the public and the Labour Party will not support the imposition of any military or economic sanctions on Germany, as, unlike Italy, they are only taking back what is theirs – a part of their country. He also says that Germany has done nothing wrong compared to Italy who have invaded Abyssinia.

What Hugh Dalton says is true because public opinion in Britain was that Germany were just taking back what was theirs and if anyone was at fault it was Italy who were doing wrong by invading Abyssinia. This opinion was shown in Britain by another MP who said, 'Germany is only moving back into her back garden'. Also when Hugh Dalton says what Germany has done is reprehensible but it is in their own frontiers he is stating a view which was commonly shared.

However, Dalton forgets to mention that Germany by re-occupying the Rhineland is breaking the Treaty of Versailles. However, public opinion in Britain about the broken Treaty was mixed. Some believed that it was wrong to break the Treaty and something should be done about it. However, some thought the Treaty was too hard in the first place on Germany.

Therefore, Hugh Dalton did reflect public opinion at the time by expressing the public view that Germany did not really do anything wrong by re-occupying the Rhineland.

(b) All the sources concentrate on three main events on the road to war and concentrate on the problems that these events caused for the British Government.

Firstly, sources A and B concentrate on the German re-occupation of the Rhineland. This was in direct contravention of the Versailles Treaty. It was Hitler's first open act of aggression. Hitler had monitored France and Britain's reactions to the Abyssinian Affair and had decided to enter into the Rhineland. The sources also highlight the British Government's attitude to this and how it reacted. The Government made only a small protest but nothing that would deter Hitler. The British saw it only as a violation of an unfair clause of the Versailles Treaty and therefore did nothing. Already Britain was having to face crises which could lead to war.

The second event dealt with by the sources is the German Anschluss with Austria. This was another big event leading up to World War Two. Germany again watched Britain and France closely before deciding to enter. Sources C and D give different views on British opinion about the Anschluss. One gives Winston Churchill's side stating that Hitler was accumulating his triumphs and territory to prepare for war whereas the other source states that Germany couldn't have been stopped except by force. Britain didn't feel that the Anschluss was serious enough to 'merit' war. The British Government had the problem of satisfying the British public yet also trying to avoid war through appeasement.

The last event dealt with in the sources is the Czechoslovak Crisis. Hitler had gotten bolder with every territorial triumph and then turned his attentions to Czechoslovakia. He firstly demanded the Sudetenland, his excuse being that he wanted to protect the Sudeten Germans but then his demands increased until he controlled all of Czechoslovakia. Sources E, F and G tell us of both the Government's opinion but also public opinion. At the Munich meeting, Hitler was appeased and told he could have the territory he wanted. At this meeting Chamberlain thought he had secured 'peace in our time'. Whereas Churchill knew that Hitler was not a man to be trusted and that he would soon increase his claims and that peace was not secure. Also Source G shows us that British citizens were not interested in what was happening in Czechoslovakia as long as it wasn't affecting them.

The sources provide a good insight into the issues facing the British Government during 1936 – 1939. The sources do not describe the actual problems – the actual events but they do give an accurate account of both the British Government's opinion and also to some extent British public opinion. The sources also highlight the consequences of the crises in the Rhineland, Austria and Czechoslovakia and give a good account of the events which in 1939 caused the outbreak of World War Two.

SECONDARY 6

Nazi thought traced through these origins can thus be summarised into four main areas: fanatical nationalism, social Darwinism, lebensraum and anti-Semitism. All of the leading Nazis were fanatical nationalists reflecting a trend that was evident in German society from the defeat of Napoleon, throughout the Second Empire and beyond the defeat and humiliation of 1918–19. This nationalism was justified in terms of social-Darwinism with the Nordic race as the racially pure survivors in the struggle with lesser breeds and negative cultures. As superior people the Germans – natural heirs to the Nordic or Aryan breed – would need to spread and be given the living space on which to expand and support themselves. This would happen at the expense of the Russians and other eastern European Slav 'untermenschen'. Thus the 'Drang nach osten' of the medieval Teutonic Knights would be fulfilled through defeat and conquest. The Jews as the negative culture, antithetical to Aryans, had plans for world domination and had stopped Germany from assuming its natural place in world order by creating 'intellect' and thus denying the power of instinct. This would have to be overcome and eliminated from a resurgent Germany.

To achieve these aims the State would have to be all encompassing and under the direction of a strong Fuhrer. Therefore although Nazism appeared to have a coherent philosophy founded on a firm basis of a recognised group of thinkers, traditional attitudes and scientific hypotheses, its key ideas were an amalgamation of carefully selected theories to suit the purposes of its proponents. Hitler said. 'One who has cultivated the art of reading will instantly discern, in a book or journal or pamphlet what ought to be remembered because it meets one's personal needs.'

This doctrine of Nazism was a collection of similar ideas sometimes taken out of context. They were moulded into the Nazi 'Weltanschauung' and once together appeared to be a coherent ideology.

But whilst Nazism could not claim to be a coherent ideology with an underlying ethical aim like Communism, it did have a set of guiding principles, however spurious or irrational these may have been.

The above responses have, of course, been removed from their original setting, viz. the assessment or test in which they figured. Secondly the questions and related sources have been omitted which, it could be argued, might make them appear meaningless and 'de-contextualised'. However, the Year Group making the responses has been identified and teachers can easily supply the missing questions from the responses given. With these caveats several key points arise.

None of the responses is perfect – blemishes are easily identifiable. Nor is it suggested that all pupils in the same year could/would make similar responses to source-based questions. Nevertheless, all responses were written during tests or assessments. Generally the length of responses increases as History courses are followed throughout the school and the sophistication of the evaluation offered increases year on year though every teacher could produce highly sophisticated responses from individual pupils in any year group. The ability to integrate source and recalled knowledge in responses and the range of language used by pupils becomes more advanced. The extract from the Certificate of Sixth Year Studies dissertation makes this point forcibly. There is a fairly marked improvement in the structure of responses offered as a pupil progresses through school with, for example, the Secondary 5 responses moving quite clearly towards reasonably well supported conclusions to the questions set. Finally, the demands made on pupils in this area of historical studies increases with courses followed.

Value of Source Evaluation in the Development of Pupil Language Skills

Historical studies make a very valuable contribution to the acquisition of language skills by pupils. Understanding and fluent use of broad historical concepts relating to social, political, economic, military, technological, religious and other developments in any age extend language skills. Similarly familiarity with such concepts as cause/effect, continuity/change, similarity/difference and stagnation/development further enhance such skills. Add to this the extended, specialised vocabulary associated with any period of history such as, for example, The Crusades, The Reformation, The Industrial Revolution, World War One or Appeasement and it will easily be recognised that the potential of historical studies as a vehicle for language development in pupils is formidable.

The progressive evaluation of sources by pupils similarly extends their use of language. Familiarisation with analysis and evaluation of sources extends pupils communication skills, adding to these a sophisticated register of language. Gradually pupils absorb and use fluently what can only be described as the language of historical scholarship. The gradual acquisition of this sophisticated language is partly seen in the pupil responses given above. Pupils become adept at absorbing the technical language of historical and literary criticism by distinguishing between primary or secondary, reliable/unreliable sources; by identifying and explaining bias in sources; by distinguishing between fact and opinion in sources; by learning to set sources in their proper historical context, by comparing viewpoints in sources, by evaluating facts and opinions in the light of events at the time or of subsequent developments. In all of these activities pupils gradually become aware of and comment on the selective nature of any historical writing.

Particular aspects of evaluating sources can extend pupil language use even further. Take for example suggesting the possible purpose for which sources were produced or written in the first place – to inform; to explain; to record; to justify; to encourage; to put forward or reflect theories, policies and plans; to approve or condemn a policy or a politician; to discuss solutions to perceived problems; to analyse views and opinions; to present information and argument; to extend or restrict understanding of a person, event or development; to approve or condemn a policy. In each of these circumstances – and only a fraction of possible purposes are referred to here – the facts or arguments used will be used selectively and betray bias. In gradually learning to detect the latter the student of History almost automatically absorbs the extended and enhanced language of historical criticism. A case can be made for drawing pupil attention to this gradual enhanced and extended use of language and encouraging pupils to move in this direction as in some of the simple activities referred to above. Acquisition of the sophisticated language of scholarship is not obviously uniquely due to the study of History but historical studies and the critical evaluation of sources make a significant contribution to this process. Familiarity with the language of scholarship is essential in the pursuit of Further or Higher Education at Colleges or Universities.

Evaluation of Sources and Other Skills Relevant to Teaching History

In arriving at a balanced evaluation of sources – a goal towards which all such evaluation exercises tend – pupils gradually learn to write structured responses to given questions. In such responses they set sources in context, analyse the content, demonstrate a body of historical knowledge related to the topics, suggest alternative views to those supplied, and support such views with relevant recalled knowledge before finally reaching a well-supported conclusion which provides a balanced judgement of the original question. In other words the relatively short, structured evaluation of sources reproduces in miniature the process expected of pupils in longer pieces of work such as the discursive historical essay. To demand a structured evaluation of sources is in fact to demand a mini-essay of students. As such source evaluation can assist in improving essay writing skills. Gathering, sorting, evaluating and reaching balanced conclusions on issues which reconciles or takes account of conflicting evidence is the very basis of essay writing and a skill much in demand in today's world. Critical evaluation of sources contributes to the acquisition of this skill.

The Way Ahead

With regard to the continued use of sources in History, their use and development in teaching is assured. This is almost certainly the case as regards the use of textual, visual and book sources in teaching. On a wider front this will be vastly expanded – indeed the process has already begun – as computers and computer technology become more available in the classroom; the present Government's promises and actions in this regard make this almost a certainty.

On the more immediate Scottish scene the Higher Still developments offer new and exciting prospects for History teaching. As such they provide an agreed framework for the study of History in Secondary 5 and Secondary 6 across the whole ability range and through the differentiated approach to learning and certification in schools. In such arrangements the use of sources will figure heavily. To all candidates, regardless of ability, Higher Still offers a wide variety of skills useful in adult life – many of these have been mentioned already – and include learning to work on your own or with others, extending the knowledge and understanding of certain aspects of the past, broadening research skills, extending writing, reading, language and communication skills, enhancing critical thinking and reasoning skills, including the ability to express and sustain logical and coherent arguments on a variety of issues. As a vehicle contributing to a student's education, the study of History has much to offer not least through the progressive evaluation of sources.

Notes

1. R.G. Collingwood, *The Idea of History*, (Oxford, 1946), p.279–280.

2. M. Lynch, *New History of Scotland*, (London, 1991), p.185.

3. See A. Cobban, *A History of Modern France*, Volume 3: 1871–1962, (London, 1965), p.79.

4. K. Mannheim, *Diagnosis of Our Time: War-Time Essays of a Sociologist*, (London, 1943). p.23.

5. H. Sharron, *Changing Children's Minds: Feuerstein's Revolution in the Teaching of Intelligence*, (London, 1987), p.36.

6. Ibid., p.44.

12

An Integrated or Discrete Approach?

Jim McGonigle

Introduction

The current debate in education, as to whether pupils in Secondary 1 and Secondary 2 in Scottish Secondary Schools, should be offered a discrete study of History, Geography and Modern Studies, or whether they should have an integrated Social Subjects curriculum, is not new. In part, the reasons for this are historical. Before 1940, History and Geography (we have to exclude Modern Studies which had yet to be developed) were usually taught as an adjunct to either English or Science. It was only in 1940 that History and Geography achieved their academic independence and claimed a discrete role in the Scottish secondary curriculum. This state of affairs was endorsed in 1947 by the then Scottish Education Department (now the Scottish Office Education and Industry Department) which resisted 'the recommendations by the Advisory Council on Education in Scotland to adopt a combined social studies approach' on the grounds that it was 'far from convinced that systematic study is outmoded'.[1]

This remained the situation until the creation, within the Social Subjects mode, of Modern Studies in 1962. The 1970s witnessed a major shake-up of the Scottish secondary curriculum. In Secondary 1 and 2, sponsored by the Consultative Committee on the Curriculum, a number of central committees were established to promote good practice in each of the subject modes. In Social Subjects, this led to the publication, in 1976, of the report from the Scottish Central Committee on Social Subjects, which concluded that 'while overall aims in Social Subjects may be broadly similar, there are differences in approach and content between the separate subjects. Each has its own logic, syntax, propositions and mode of enquiry. Each offers a distinctive kind of mental structuring'.[2] This report goes on to state that 'the Committee wishes to affirm its support for the continuance of the disciplines within the field of Social Subjects'.[3]

However, the 1980s witnessed a massive structural shift in the secondary curriculum. Knowledge and skills per se were no longer sufficient for pupils who would be leaving school and entering a free enterprise economy. Vocational application of curriculum subjects became the norm. If your subject could not modernise and show how its unique set of skills, values and body of knowledge could be applied to the world of work, then it deserved to go the same way as the dinosaurs. This was the age of the Technical and Vocational Education Initiative (TVEI).

In this period, the discrete subjects at last abandoned (indeed were forced to abandon in order to survive) their isolationist attitudes towards each other. Gone, to a certain extent, was the competition at the end of Secondary 2 for numbers for Secondary 3 which would merit the retention of a fellow colleague. Staff began to discuss the positive contribution which the component elements of History, Geography and Modern Studies could bring to a pupil's learning experience, as well as the enrichment offered by a coherent Social Subjects curriculum.

It was in this atmosphere that pressure was beginning to mount for an integrated course in Secondary 1 and 2. Articles by the likes of John MacVicar in the Times Educational Supplement Scotland, in which he claimed that 'the existing provision left much to be desired',[4] merely added to the pressure on subject departments and gave increased fire-power to senior management teams which were questioning 'the validity of the smaller departments'.[5]

However, as a group, and with far-reaching structural changes in the curriculum, and an attitudinal change towards fellow Social Subjects teachers, the Social Subjects responded to the challenges raised.

In a sense, this was formally recognised in 1989 with the publication, by the Scottish Consultative Council on the Curriculum, of *Curriculum Design for the Secondary Stages*, (the so-called Yellow Peril) in which the Social Subjects were grouped under one mode and allocated 10 per cent of time available in the secondary school week.

Once more, the issue of how Social Subjects should be taught has arisen in the 1990s from a variety of sources. Her Majesty's Inspectorate are pushing from the angle of raising standards and levels of achievement, as well as pressing for courses which challenge the more able. However, it should be noted that in the foreword to the report, *Achieving Success in Secondary 1 and 2*, Her Majesty's Senior Chief Inspector, Douglas Osler, concludes, 'the report recommends no fundamental structural change to education at Secondary 1 and 2'.[6]

In addition to the above, Social Subjects departments have to fulfil the demands of the 5–14 development programme for Environmental Studies. Further, there are individuals, like Brian Boyd, Head of Quality in Education at Jordanhill Campus, Glasgow, who is demanding a restructuring of the Secondary 1 and 2 curriculum to ensure coherence and progression from Primary 7 to Secondary 1, with a concomitant reduction in the number of teachers to which new Secondary 1 pupils are exposed.

Such is the state of the debate at present. But, what are the arguments behind the proposal of an integrated Social Subjects curriculum and, more importantly, how valid are these arguments? This chapter analyses these arguments and tests their validity. (It should be noted at this point, that for the purposes of this chapter, a discrete methodology and mode of delivery is one whereby a pupil is taught by a subject specialist teacher in individual, subject-based departments. An integrated course is one where one Social Subjects teacher would teach all the components of the Social Subjects course, irrespective of their subject background and training. Further exemplification of the various approaches which can be adopted, are to be found in the report, *The Social Subjects in Secondary Schools*, Curriculum Paper 15, HMSO, (Edinburgh, 1976) Appendix B, p.74.)

To Integrate or Not

To begin this section it is necessary to take a small step backwards, to examine how History is delivered in the primary sector. In the main, and until the advent of the 5–14 development programme for Environmental Studies, History was subsumed into a more integrated and less subject based approach. This style of teaching has been greatly influenced by the contribution of psychologists as to the best mode of delivery and curriculum development. Foremost amongst these are the broad stages of cognitive development defined by Piaget. These can be summarised as follows:

STAGE	AGE NORMS
Sensorimotor	0–2
Pre-operational	
(a) pre-conceptual thought	2–4
(b) intuitive thought	4–7
Operational	
(a) concrete operational thought	7–11
(b) formal operational thought	11–16

This line of thought has led to the conclusion that 'History can be difficult for primary pupils – or for those who have not reached Piaget's formal operational thinking – simply because it cannot be experienced directly'.[7] Although with the evolution of the 5–14 development programme, the focus of History teaching has moved more towards a more discrete, rather than integrated approach, the fact remains that History, in the primary school, is taught, as defined by Her Majesty's Inspectorate, by 'a single, generalist teacher'.[8] It is from this standpoint that the arguments follow that, as in primary, so in secondary, History should be taught as part of an integrated Social Subjects curriculum.

However, as early as 1922, Oakden and Sturt had argued that, between the ages of 8–11, children's temporal understanding develops markedly; by the ages of 8–9, 'children accurately use the terms past, present, and future and are able to correctly associate people and events with these terms'.[9] They continue, 'at ages 8–9, children are beginning to master historical dates; place events in sequence and to associate dates with particular people and events. From 9–11, children begin to label periods of time'.[10]

Consequently, the argument for integration begins to look somewhat suspect and is further undermined by research in 1982, conducted by Harner, which suggested that children by the age of 10–12, have mastered 'the varied linguistic structures related to time'.[11]

It must be borne in mind that at the time of transfer to Secondary Schools in Scotland, pupils are aged between 11 and 12 when, as the evidence suggests, pupils are able to handle and 'develop skills such as critical thinking, debate and source-based evaluation and investigating'.[12] In addition, Thornton and Vukelich observed in 1988 that 'new time words learnt in early adolescence are mainly derived from learning the subject of History. The development of concepts such as generation, epoch and century are dependent on direct instruction'.[13]

This evidence demonstrates that in the upper stages of Primary School 'History gives young people not just knowledge, but the tools to reflect on, critically to evaluate and to apply their knowledge'.[14] To an extent, this research has recently influenced thinking at the highest levels within Scottish education with the assertion that 'at the upper stages of primary schools, consideration should be given to whether all aspects of the curriculum should be taught by a single, generalist teacher'.[15]

Thus, evidence from recent research argues that 'History furnishes the skills, insights and knowledge'[16] to young people and that these skills can be mastered at an earlier age. Hence, the argument that the Primary School model should be adopted in secondary is a non sequitur.

As to the arguments advanced by John MacVicar et al , that Social Subjects should be taught as an 'holistic type of course',[17] the main thrust of the debate seems to be based on time-table constraints, finance (or lack of it) and the impact of falling school rolls. He, too, is of the opinion that the primary experience can be successfully replicated in Secondary 1 and 2.

However, an important caveat should be borne in mind about the very public debate concerning the future of History. As John Slater trenchantly argued, public debate on History is 'political, as it is driven, strengthened and sometimes grievously distorted, by organisations (and authors), aiming not only to strengthen their own ideas but also to persuade politicians to strengthen or change theirs'.[18]

Such a point of view could also be said to apply to the lobby, led by Brian

Boyd. The concern here, once again, is not with the quality of the curriculum on offer, but the sheer quantity of it and the myriad ways in which it is presented, stating that the Social Subjects should be delivered as an integrated package, with one teacher delivering all the component parts – in order to reduce the number of talking heads to which pupils in Secondary 1 are currently exposed. It does not appear to matter that in pupil surveys, this facet of life in secondary schools is consistently highly rated by those same Secondary 1 pupils. Admittedly, the evidence for this is, at best, empirical. Year on year surveys of Secondary 1 pupils in the author's school highlight the fact that pupils in Secondary 1 enjoy the change of teachers, the varied teaching methodologies to which they are exposed, and indeed, the movement from class to class. The survey of 1997 showed that 67 per cent of the pupils commented positively on this aspect of their secondary education. Now, the pupils are not *vox populi, vox dei*, but, in this educational consumerist society in which we live, the views of the consumers have to be given some credence.

However as early as 1976, arguments to counter those now being used, had already been promulgated:

> In avoiding disciplines, in attempting to transcend them to some newer and more general level of synthesis, the teacher may seek some quick and seemingly total route to knowledge. Instruction cast in this mould leads away from ideas, from clear language, from productive models of thought and from the simplicity and order of thought, all of which can be more readily attained through the disciplines.[19]

Further evidence from the 1980s undermines the integrationist argument. In a submission to the Consultative Committee on the Curriculum (now the Scottish Consultative Committee on the Curriculum), Dr McNicholl concluded that since 'some subject-based objectives are not readily subsumed within a unified statement, these provided an argument for the retention of the discrete subject bases'.[20] In this same report, it was recommended that an integrated Secondary 1 and 2 course is 'not advocated'[21] for the following reason:

> the fact that (the) objectives are more satisfactorily expressed in subject-specific terms, strengthens the view that the separate identity of the contributing subject bases should be preserved.[22]

In acknowledging the fundamental place in teaching and learning of properly qualified teachers, the report commented:

> the situation where teachers normally teach subjects in which they are academically qualified and appropriately trained, is regarded as one of the strengths of the Scottish system and should be preserved.[23]

The quality of many integrated courses on offer in Secondary 1 and 2 has been questioned by Her Majesty's Inspectorate who reported that 'the effectiveness of such courses would not justify their widespread introduction across the curriculum'.[24] Furthermore, 'such a move (integrated courses) could mean that pupils would lose not only the benefits of access to staff with specialist knowledge and skills, but also the opportunity to begin the study in depth of disciplines which have stood the test of time and which will form the basis of later study'.[25]

One school, where an integrated approach for the humanities was introduced in session 1996/1997, is Stranraer Academy. The rationale for this course was 'to create greater curriculum coherence through contact with fewer teachers'.[26] Proponents of this course argue that the problem in achieving a coherence across the curriculum from Primary 7 to Secondary 2 originates in the way in which secondary schools are structured – that is, in discrete subject areas. The benefits of this approach to integration appeared to be a greater knowledge of pupils as a result of the increased number of contacts per week allowed under the new structure, and a more effective monitoring of attendance and the use of the school homework diary. However, the report on this integrated course does not evaluate the extent to which it led to greater depth of subject knowledge and understanding than can be offered by the discrete subject approach. Indeed, the findings of this report made no mention of such an end. The evidence is hardly persuasive or overwhelming for the whole scale abandonment of the status quo in favour of what Lord Derby would have described as 'a leap in the dark'.

In this period, when so much of educational debate is focused on the promotion of 'high expectations of the attainment of pupils',[27] it does not follow logically that this aim can be achieved by a dilution and diminution of the quality of the learning experience which is provided by subject-specialist teachers in their discrete subject disciplines.

It could be concluded that the arguments advanced so far are largely negative – that is, they explain why a discrete approach is preferable to an integrated one. To an extent, that is correct. The next section, however, will look at the compelling arguments advanced for a discrete, subject-discipline mode of curriculum delivery.

Maintaining the Discrete Approach

In order to argue the case for the maintenance of the discrete subject delivery of History, a brief look at the contribution which History makes to the pupils' learning experience and to the broader curriculum is necessary. Abundant evidence and research exist to justify the place of History in the curriculum. In 1972 Burston argued:

the distinctive benefit of historical study lies in the understanding of the past which it gives us and which, if applied to the present, will aid our understanding of the contemporary world in a way that no other subject can.[28]

Burston's argument was supported by Sir Keith Joseph in his advocacy of History as a separate subject:

> In the study of History, and no where else, the chief objective is to enable pupils to gain some understanding of human activity in the past and its implications for the present. They (the pupils) will be caused to think about continuity and change, similarity and differences, in a way and in a context quite different from their encounter with these concepts in other subjects.[29]

Again, in 1993, in their report on *Effective Teaching and Learning, History,* Her Majesty's Inspectorate stated that 'History provides insights and a sense of perspective which are essential to an understanding of the contemporary world and it makes a distinctive contribution to the curriculum'.[30]

This view is supported by Buck, Iman and Moorse who emphasised the importance of an historical perspective without which 'we lack a crucial way of looking at and understanding human society'.[31]

Indeed, in the report *Achieving Success in Secondary 1 and 2,* an obligation is placed upon History staff and departments to ensure that 'pupils who do not study History beyond Secondary 2 should have established a substantial framework of historical skills and understanding which will remain with them into adult life'.[32] No other subject in this report has such an onus placed on it for pupils who do not continue with that particular subject beyond Secondary 2.

As can be seen, the case for the inclusion of History in the curriculum is well made and well documented. But, the aim here is not to justify the inclusion of History in the Scottish secondary curriculum, but to maintain its distinct and discrete mode of delivery.

The quotations above show what role History has to offer pupils in Scottish schools. The contention is that such a role can only be fulfilled by the use of subject specialists delivering a sophisticated course which ensures coherence and balance, and where the learning objectives are clearly identified, and understood, in a discrete subject mode. History plays a fundamental role in establishing pupils' 'commitment to those values that are fundamental to the democratic way of life'.[33]

This responsibility is too great to be left to chance. The History teacher has to combine the transmission of knowledge, an understanding of what gives that knowledge significance with a parallel development of the skills which are necessary and used by pupils to interpret knowledge and ideas with confidence and independence. As a historian, the History teacher also has a responsibility 'to avoid bias both in the selection of the evidence and in its presentation and interpretation, and this is particularly difficult to discharge'.[34] This burden is too great to be discharged by a non-subject specialist.

To develop what could be called the value of History, the subject helps to develop a series of skills and insights related to the evaluation of evidence by asking the question, 'how do I know this is true?' It helps to develop empathy by demanding answers to 'what was it like to be?' and 'what would I have done if?' Finally, by its very nature of discussion and justification of conclusions based on evidence, the values of History reflect the values of an open society. This point was brought home forcefully to the author a number of years ago. The author was teaching the daughter of a fellow colleague, and on asking how Secondary 1 was doing, the girl replied enthusiastically that all was going well. On further discussion, it emerged that History was her favourite subject. When asked to explain, she replied, 'They talk to you, let you discuss and value your opinion'. By its nature, History is an endless debate. To deprive pupils of this element is to do them a great disservice.

Indeed, this theme was the subject of a recent international conference in Braunchsweig, reported in the *Times Educational Supplement Scotland* on 23 June 1998. The author, Hilary Cooper, concluded that, 'the French treat History as dogma. The Germans learn it by rote, and the Spanish are hung up on chronology. But British History teachers are taking a lead in treating it as a living subject, demanding objective analysis'. It is this idea of History as a 'living subject' which would be lost in an integrated approach.

History, therefore, is not merely about the transmission of a body of knowledge or a collection of facts – if that were the case, it could be argued that there should be a return to the pre-1940 scenario where History was an addendum to English – which would justify an integrated approach. But, as Clare Hake and Terry Haydn remind us, there is much more to the teaching of History nowadays:

> the ability to explain an aspect of the past in a clear and engaging manner is still a central part of the art of the History teacher. It forms connections between sources and accounts and explanations which is essential if children are to make sense of the past.[35]

Her Majesty's Inspector L. MacCallum emphasises the essential attributes of the successful History teacher who has the ability 'to fascinate children by employing a wide range of historical knowledge and interesting anecdotes, by using local and modern parallels, related to children's own experiences, by posing interesting questions and to make them think'.[36]

The incident comes to mind of a young Secondary 1 pupil, led into the author's class by the Headteacher, having been found running in the corridor to get to his class. When questioned as to the reason for this breach of school regulations, the young waif replied, 'But sir, we're killing Wallace today'! No other colleague has this difficulty!

Such a depth of experience and skill cannot be subsumed into the general art of teaching. These values reflect the distinct ways in which historians and History teachers are trained, and it is these same skills and mores of which children would be bereft in a pastiche of a Social Subjects integrated curriculum. As Bruner argues: 'there is nothing more central to a discipline than its way of thinking. The best introduction to a subject is the subject itself. The task of saying what a subject is about, its own way of thinking, its modes of procedure, the definition of its aims and objectives, may best be performed by the specialist teacher'.[37]

Bruner's argument is developed in the 5–14 development programme which recognises the importance of developing a sense of time. This does not come automatically and 'has to be consciously taught and developed if young people are to move beyond the simple description of the past as a vague, undifferentiated time called olden days'.[38] This, surely, is best achieved by deploying the skills of the specialist History teacher who has the 'experience and knowledge to help children to articulate their existing knowledge and connecting them with new learning'.[39]

History is further distinguished as a discipline by 'the questions historians ask and the way they ask them, as well as the ability to interpret evidence through a process of deductive reasoning'.[40] This is the particular slant which History teachers bring to their subject which demands the retention of a discrete subject approach and this interactionist role 'implies that teachers need subject discipline knowledge and the ability to make appropriate interventions in order to scaffold children's learning'.[41]

It has been argued that History is thus more than the mere acquisition of knowledge to be accepted without argument or debate. What gives it life is the premise of discussion and dispute over the concepts of change and continuity, and cause and effect which are central to the understanding of why an event happened or helps to evaluate its impact. It is this elan vital which is the realm of the subject specialist. However, History has other contributions to make to the experience of the school child.

Additional benefits of History courses have been highlighted by authors as diverse as Sir Keith Joseph and Buck, Iman and Moorse. In his address to the 1989 Historical Association London Conference on History, Sir Keith Joseph, then Secretary of State for Education in England and Wales, stressed the importance of what have become known as 'transferable skills':

> skills acquired through the study of History can also enhance young peoples' use of language, numeracy, observation and communication with other people. History is also indispensable to understanding the society we live in.[42]

At the same conference, John Slater argued that, 'by transmitting the values of society, History teaching can contribute to their perpetuation'.[43] Buck, Iman and Moorse go further, arguing for a History which is 'explicitly underpinned by dimensions, skills and themes, will have much to contribute to the personal and social development of pupils'.[44]

Such a theme, of the wider contribution of History to the pupils' learning experience, was explored in a Europe-wide project, the Phare/Tacis Project, funded by the European Union – and involving six countries, of which Scotland was one. The project theme was the promotion of democratic values through the teaching of History – a clear vindication of the central role which History can play in the formation of national characteristics. The differing approaches of the participating nations were revealing, ranging from the Danish democratic tradition of allowing pupils to negotiate History topics for study with their teachers, with the implicit recognition of the needs for a specialist teacher with specialist subject knowledge, to the government orthodoxy expected in the Slovak republic. The approaches may have differed, but all the participants agreed that the role of History and the History specialist teacher, should be to encourage debate, listen to other points of view, reach conclusions based on available evidence and to foster a willingness to alter viewpoints in the light of new evidence.

These ideas may appear to be over-ambitious to the casual observer, but they form part of the armoury which the History specialist has acquired and which are implicit in, and underpin, the delivery of the History curriculum in Secondary 1 and 2. What a disservice would be done to our young people if all were not able to benefit from that approach and experience.

To return to the central theme of this chapter, should History continue to be taught as a discrete subject or should it be part of an integrated Secondary 1 and 2 Social Subjects course?

If the aim or assumption behind an integrated course is that each component can be distilled into chunks of knowledge and a body of skills to be mastered, then there is no reason to doubt that such an objective could be achieved via the medium of an integrated course. However, if it is accepted that the aim of teaching History is broader in scope than this narrow interpretation – in the words of Her Majesty's Inspectorate report on *Effective Teaching and Learning, History*, that 'History provides insights and a sense of perspective essential to an understanding of the contemporary world',[45] then a subject specialist, discrete discipline approach is not only needed but essential. This same report argues, as have others, that History makes a distinct contribution to the curriculum[46] but goes further in enjoining History teachers to 'foster an interest in History which will provide a lifelong source of enjoyment'.[47]

Such a responsibility can also be found in the rationale for Standard Grade,

Higher, Certificate of Sixth Year Studies, and the proposed Higher Still History Conditions and Arrangements published by the Scottish Qualifications Authority. The aim of lifelong enjoyment is fostered by the creation of 'conditions which motivate pupils to make sustained progress in learning within a common curricular framework'.[48]

In *The Principles of History Teaching*, Burston summed up the key arguments:

> any attempt to synthesise the whole of History and Geography into a single course risks losing the intellectual discipline and educational benefit of either.[49]

Conclusion

Despite the powerful arguments for a discrete approach, History teachers must be sensitive to the public debate and be positive in their response to it. In order to maintain the discrete approach, they must seek to demonstrate that such an approach can 'reconcile the breadth of the curriculum with the dangers of fragmentation where pupils follow too many courses'.[50]

This can be achieved by close collaboration with fellow Social Subject disciplines to ensure that there is continuity, coherence, and progression in the learning environment of pupils. A further solution comes in blocking and rotating the Social Subjects in the timetable. Frank Cooney, Head of Social Studies at Northern College, has rightly criticised what he describes as, 'the discrete delivery of one period a week (of History, Geography and Modern Studies) with no co-operation between social subjects', which he goes on to call, 'a recipe for disaster which justifies all the complaints by education officials and critics of social subjects'.[51]

His solution supports the idea of rotation – ensuring pupils have one Social Subject teacher at a time, allowing for greater in-depth study and at the same time, developing a greater teacher/pupil understanding. This approach is one way by which History and fellow Social Subjects teachers can demonstrate their awareness of demands for change. Blocking and rotating the social subjects is clearly advocated in *Achieving Success in Secondary 1 and 2* which gives 'teachers a better chance to get to know their pupils and to consolidate knowledge and skills through more frequent contact with pupils'.[52]

By adopting such a strategy (if it does not at present exist), History teachers, in collaboration with their Social Subject colleagues, will be able to justify the confidence shown in them by Her Majesty's Inspectorate, who conclude that 'there is no compelling case, at present, for a radical re-organisation of the Secondary 1 and 2 curriculum'.[53]

It is up to the History profession to justify that confidence!

Notes

1. The Social Subjects in Secondary Schools – Curricular Paper 15 HMSO, (Edinburgh, 1976), p.7.

2. Ibid., p.11.

3. Ibid., p.13.

4. J. MacVicar, 'Getting Together', *Times Educational Supplement Scotland*', 27/1/1984.

5. Ibid.

6. Her Majesty's Inspector of Schools, Achieving Success in Secondary 1 and 2, (Edinburgh, 1997) p.4.

7. Curricular Paper 15, p.9.

8. Achieving Success in Secondary 1 and 2, p.16.

9. E.C. Oakden and M. Sturt, 'Development of knowledge of time in children'. Quoted in C.A. Simchowitz, 'The development of temporal concepts in children and its significance', *Teaching History*, April 1995, p.15.

10. Ibid.

11. W. Friedman, (ed), *The Development of Psychology of Time,* (New York, 1982).

12. Duncan Toms, 'History's future lies in classroom debate', *Times Educational Supplement Scotland*, 31/1/1996

13. S.J. Thornton and R. Vukelich, 'Effects of children's understanding of time concepts on historical understanding', *Theory and Research in Social Education*, Volume XVI, 1988.

14. John Slater, *The Politics of History Teaching – A Humanity Dehumanised*, (London, 1988), p.8.

15. Achieving Success in Secondary 1 and 2, p.16.

16. John Slater, The Politics of History Teaching, p.6.

17. J. MacVicar, Getting Together, *Times Educational Supplement Scotland*.

18. John Slater, The Politics of History Teaching, p.3.

19. Curricular Paper 15, p.78.

20. Consultative Council on the Curriculum, Curriculum Guidelines for Secondary 1 and 2 Social Subjects, (Edinburgh, 1986), p.50.

21. Ibid., p.1

22. Ibid., p.10

23. Ibid., p.50

24. Achieving Success in Secondary 1 and 2, p.12

25. Ibid., p.12.

26. B. Bryant and C. Rigg, 'An integrated approach for humanities in S1', Unpublished Report, Stranraer, 1997.

27. Achieving Success in Secondary 1 and 2, p.29.

28. W.H. Burston, *The Principles of History Teaching*, (London, 1972), p.211.

29. Keith Joseph, 'Why teach History in schools?, quoted in *The Historian*, Volume 2, London, 1989.

30. Effective Teaching and Learning in Scottish Secondary Schools, Scottish Office Education Department, 1992, p.2.

31. M. Buck, S. Iman and K. Moorse, 'Educating the Whole Child', Historical Association Occasional Paper Number 10, (London 1994), p.5.

32. Achieving Success in Secondary 1 and 2, p.14.

33. Scottish Examination Board, Standard Grade Conditions and Arrangements, Edinburgh, 1988.

34. Keith Joseph, 'Why Teach History?'

35. C. Hake and T. Haydn, 'Stories or Sources?', *Teaching History*, January 1995, p.22.

36. L. MacCallum, Effective Teaching and Learning – History – Conference Report, (HMSO 1994), p.10.

37. J.S. Bruner, *The Relevance of Education*, (London, 1972).

38. Social Subjects, Understanding People in the Past, Scottish Consultative Council on the Curriculum, 1996, p.10.

39. E. Wood and C. Holden, 'I can't remember doing Romans', *Teaching History*, October 1997, p.9.

40. H. Cooper, *The Teaching of History*, (London, 1992), quoted in Wood and Holden.

41. Wood and Holden, 'I can't remember', p.11.

42. Keith Joseph, 'Why Teach History?'

43. John Slater, 'The Case for History in School', *The Historian*, Vol.2, 1989, p.16.

44. M. Buck, S. Iman and K. Moorse, 'Educating the Whole Child', p.14.

45. Effective Teaching and Learning, History, p.2.

46. Ibid., p.3.

47. Ibid., p.6.

48. Achieving Success in Secondary 1 and 2, p.39.

49. W.H. Burston, *The Principles of History Teaching*, p.209.

50. Achieving Success in Secondary 1 and 2, p.8.

51. Frank Cooney, 'Dinosaurs Bite Back', *Times Educational Supplement Scotland*, 17/4/1998.

52. Achieving Success in Secondary 1 and 2, p.12.

53. Ibid., p.17.

Index

Index

Index